"The events of our lives point to underlying patterns, which can teach us to find our place in an unfolding future. *The Path of Synchronicity* gently tasks readers to first notice the mysterious aspects of our lives and then to descend into Self to discern how our individual experiences enhance or hinder living in flow with the synchronous energies of the cosmos… a timely and groundbreaking guide."

—JULIE CLAYTON,
New Consciousness Review

"Oxford graduate, therapist, and professor of literature Hunter has combined his unique skill set to create one of the most comprehensive discussions of the descent into the darkness of the subconscious which I have ever read. He doesn't just tell readers how to get there, and what they can expect to find once they have arrived, but he specifically details the intricacies of mining the treasures at those depths in order to proceed along the path of spiritual and psychic transformation. Chapter titles in Part One (the explanation section) include The Guiding Hand, Head Versus Heart, and Synchronicity in Literature. Part Two (the part about dealing with obstacles in the the land of the shadow self) has titles such as Mind Traps and How We Construct Reality, Refusing the Flow, Expect Help Along the Way, and The Eight Barriers to Synchronicity. Dynamic and well-written, this one is a standout in the field."

—ANNA JEDRZIEWSKI,
New Age Retailer

THE PATH OF
SYNCHRONICITY
ALIGN YOURSELF WITH YOUR LIFE'S FLOW

Dr. Allan G. Hunter

FINDHORN PRESS

Findhorn Press
One Park Street
Rochester, Vermont 05767
www.findhornpress.com

Findhorn Press is a division of Inner Traditions International

ISBN 978-1-84409-539-1

Cataloging-in-Publication Data for this title is available from the British Library

Printed and bound in the United States

Edited by Nicky Leach
Cover, text design and layout by Damian Keenan

CONTENTS

CONTENTS

Part Two - The Obstacles to Synchronicity

CONTENTS

For C.C.B., with love

Acknowledgments

Inevitably when the topic is synchronicity it's hard to be quite sure where to start thanking people, since so many have appeared, ready to help me, and seemingly by miraculous intervention. But I'm going to try anyway. Findhorn Press publisher Thierry Bogliolo certainly takes first place here, since it was as a direct result of conversations with him, and thanks to his nudging, that I felt spurred to write about synchronous events as they appeared in literature and history. Without him this book could not have happened, and his friendship is one I treasure.

Once I started writing, various people came to my aid and support in ways that also deserve recognition and gratitude. Baptist de Pape, with his ever-penetrating inquiries into the topic, helped me enormously as I moved forward, as did Bonnie David, Miriam Knight, and Lilou Macé.

My students, in their open discussions of the way fate works in literature, were always my most challenging helpers, and I'd like to single out Brittany Capozzi, Laura Cluff, and Samantha Crescitelli, particularly, for their insights and wisdom.

Others who were of considerable help, and who are dear friends, include David Whitley (Cambridge University), and Andrew Peerless (Oxford University Press). Anna Portnoy and Nick Portnoy were also enormously supportive, and loaned me the courage to take the plunge and write more about what I knew. In every case, their comments produced more insights as I went forward.

I would like to thank, also, Mrs. Arline Greenleaf and her daughter Mrs. Rebecca Greenleaf Clapp, and the board of the Seth Sprague Educational and Charitable Foundation, for their continued support, which allowed me to explore the ideas expressed in these pages as part of an examination of literature and the way writers have approached the idea of fate.

In addition, Curry College continued to support my writing in various indirect ways, and I am happy to thank its president, Ken Quigley; its board of trustees; CAO

David Potash; Deans Pennini and Ijiri; my colleagues, Paula Cabral, Professors Jeffrey Di Iuglio, Jeannette DeJong, Marcy Holbrook, and Dr. Ronald Warners for their input and inspiration. Beyond the campus of Curry College, Daniel Davis, Nora Klaver, Paula Ogier, Michel Lavoie, and Suzanne Strempek Shea were significant in their great-hearted and patient support of my endeavors.

My greatest debt, as always, is to Cat Bennett. Not only did our conversations enrich my understanding but I was privileged to see synchronous events unfolding in her own life, which then allowed me to observe my own experience with fresh eyes.

To Gail Torr, my hard-working and delightful publicist, and to Nicky Leach, my inspired and inspiring editor, I send gratitude in quantities that can never be large enough. Damian Keenan deserves special thanks for his splendid design work. And Carol Shaw, Sabine Weeke, Mieke Wik, and all at Findhorn Press have a special place in my heart for all their care and devotion over the years.

Good deeds never end; and gratitude never ends, either.

"A Funny Thing Happened..."

Two days after I'd finished what I thought was the final draft of this book, the new collaborative book by well-known spiritual gurus Deepak Chopra, Debbie Ford, and Marianne Williamson entitled *The Shadow Effect* was published. I was surprised; especially as I'd just decided I wanted to call my new book "Synchronicity, the Shadow, and You." I'd spent some years coming to grips with the meaning of the Shadow, dissatisfied by most of what I'd read about the topic; then, suddenly, here were three major authors launching a book on exactly the same subject.

Obviously, I rushed out, bought it, and read it the same day.

I found that what they had to say was wonderful, and I recommend their book to anyone; yet, even though we deal with many of the same issues, their book is very different from what these pages contain. I feel they missed certain vital information. But we do agree on the main point: the Shadow—that unacknowledged part of each of us that can subvert so many of our best impulses—is an important topic, and understanding it offers us a way out of self-thwarting and self-destructive acts.

After I'd closed their book, a realization hit me. This was an exact reflection of the nature of synchronicity, because the essence of synchronicity is that we have a choice as to how we respond to it. Two linked events had occurred at the same time, and in doing so had presented me with a choice. One reaction open to me was to feel disappointed that "my" topic seemed to have been preempted. But that would have been a rather silly, ego-based reaction, because it's not "my" topic any more than the sky is mine; the ego is always looking for a chance to feel slighted.

However, there was another option open to me, and I took it. I recognized that this event was a real blessing. With several books out on the subject, more people would now be far more open to the idea that the Shadow deserved serious exploration. This would be good for readers everywhere, especially those who wrestle unsuccessfully with their darker impulses on a daily basis.

So here is the point: if we regard synchronicity as chance, or luck, then it could be good or bad, depending upon our mind frame at the time. But if we see an event like this as part of a larger pattern—in this case a pattern that allows more people to join a discussion about a vital topic—then we can see that it's not about "my" book or "your" book, or who wrote what first, but about what the world needs to look at more closely. The ego, of course, doesn't like being part of a pattern. It wants to be center stage. So it disregards anything that doesn't add to its importance. That's why my ego-self wanted to have a hissy fit.

When synchronous events occur, in fact, they pose some rather difficult questions. For if we admit that synchronicity exists then we have to accept that there is a purpose to life, that there is a divinity that shapes our destinies, and that we may have a purpose on Earth that is bigger than our next shopping trip. The ego doesn't care for this line of thinking, since that would put its own clamorous demands in second place. The ego wants to keep asking for things to make it feel important, not to cede pride of place to a pattern, even a divine one. So it tries to convince us there's no such thing.

And that is how synchronicity works—by testing us. An event happens, it coincides with another event, and at that point we have a choice: we can either discount both events or we can see that perhaps there is a pattern emerging. And then we have to trust that the pattern is a useful one. If we can hold on to this trust then events tend to lead on to other events. We enter a flow that is simply not perceptible to doubters.

In the pages that follow we'll explore this process, and we'll see that part of it, at its deepest level, requires that we must seek to understand the Shadow. Without understanding the Shadow, we cannot get into the full flow of synchronicity—that series of seemingly miraculous coincidences where open door leads to open door in our lives. The Shadow works with the ego to try and stop this happening, for if I am working for a cause that is greater than me, then I can't be working for the ego as well. Since it doesn't see anything as more important than itself, this represents a crisis for the ego. The ego responds by saying "that's not fair!" It calls upon the feeling of anger that lurks within the Shadow, and in response it will rage at us, making all sorts of trouble. It will cause so much chaos that if we don't face our Shadow and learn how to deal with it we'll discover that we simply won't be able to grasp synchronicity. The Shadow will make us blind and deaf to it. And yet, once we have taken the Shadow into account, once we see how it operates, it seems as if synchronicities open up all the time.

To show how it all works I've relied on several sources of material. The first is the observed experiences of those I have taught and counseled for over 30 years, and also my own experiences of synchronicity. The second source, which backs up the first, comes from 3,000 years of myth, legend, and literature, much of which depicts psychic processes that mirror the processes my clients and students go through.

As people move toward a sense of personal authenticity and living life in the flow of synchronicity, they live through—in one form or another—versions of many of the great stories and legends of our culture. That so much literature, for so long, has been concerned with the same issues of synchronicity and fate, and in the same way, is convincing evidence that synchronicity exists. In each case, the main characters have had to struggle with the ego and the Shadow in order to move into alignment with synchronicity—or Fate, or Destiny, as it is sometimes called. Literature and myth provide abundant and convincing evidence that this is a concept central to the shared human psyche, one that Carl Jung called "The Collective Unconscious."

By looking at both sets of evidence, personal and literary, we'll see that living fully with synchronicity depends upon several things. First of all we have to notice that aspects of our lives are mysterious, that there seems to be a synchronous pattern, and we must let ourselves be curious about this. Then we have to allow ourselves to descend into the self to find out more about who we are. Some people never go on this journey, and that is ultimately their loss.

This idea of the descent, during which we meet the Shadow self, is a repeated feature of literature and myth, and one of its most compelling aspects. It's a well-traveled path in its general form, except that everyone's path is individual. No one's path is ever exactly the same as anyone else's. Perhaps that's why we have so many tales about this. The trip to the underworld appears in the tales of Odysseus, Orpheus, Persephone, the Buddha, Jesus, Dante, Sir Gawain, King Lear, Hamlet, and many others, including the contemporary tale of Harry Potter. Our ancestors would have been well aware of this motif, just as we talk familiarly of having "dark nights of the soul,"[1] when we go through a time of personal soul-searching.

If we undertake this inward journey, we are forced to ask questions about our personal beliefs and values. Inevitably, this leads us to take a new look at our moral world and admit our frailties. And when we do meet our Shadow Self, we discover that it has the potential to become a source of real power that will awaken us to our deep compassion—if we do not flee from it. Once we've learned from this encounter we have to reemerge and live that wisdom, trusting in it. This, in turn, will open our eyes to an awareness of how synchronicity truly operates in our lives and a sense of how we can move with it.

If this sounds rather abstract, don't worry. The journey has been described by Homer, Dante, Shakespeare, and others in ways you'll find easy to comprehend, even if you haven't read these writers since high school. No separate technical language exists to describe what psychic transformation looks like and feels. These processes can only be apprehended through metaphor, relayed through the stories we know as myth and literature.

On a personal note, I admit to knowing a certain amount about synchronicity first hand. I've already given one example, and I'll add that this book wouldn't let me rest until I'd written it. In truth, all my books followed that pattern, coming to me demanding that I write them. Events would keep piling up until I had to respond. It felt as though each day I'd be handed another piece of information that helped me on my path.

I make no claim to superior or esoteric learning. I do know, however, about the descent into the deep self because I've done it and helped others tackle that journey, too. The resulting gift this experience hands to each of us is that it allows us to live more fully in the mythic dimension of life.

And so, as I wrote these pages, I trusted the synchronicities that came my way, one at a time, one day at a time, permitting me to see just far enough forward to do what needed to be done, to say what needed to be said. That's the way synchronicity works. It uses us to get done what needs to be done, and we can't always see the end result—simply because we're human.

This may lead you think that I'm too limited, too unreliable to write for others. So let me put it this way: a signpost does not have to be made of gold—it just has to point the right way.

Part One
What is Synchronicity?

CHAPTER 1

Synchronicity or Just Dumb Luck?

The Three Things We Must Do

Most of us have noticed them—those moments when things go just exactly right. These are the times when the right person turns up at exactly the perfect moment to save the situation—those occasions when it feels as if the stars have aligned miraculously to move you to where you need to be. You can call it luck, or karma, or coincidence, or the Guiding Hand, the Universe, or God. You could thank your Guardian Angel, the spirit of your ancestors, your patron saint, or simply call it a miracle.

Sometimes we call this the blessing of "friends." We look at our dearest friend of dozens of years and know that we couldn't have trodden the path we did without that person's help. He or she was exactly the person we needed. That friend may well be a miraculous gift.

We have plenty of words we can use to attempt to describe this. But how do we understand it? And if we understand it, then what do we do about it?

The day after I got married, my wife and I boarded a plane for England, and, for the first and only time in my life in which I've made hundreds of flights, we were upgraded for free to first class. We sprawled in our luxurious leather seats, sipped champagne, and felt blessed. Simple luck, perhaps? Or a hint from the Universe?

Then there is Bob M., an independent bookstore owner and a friend of mine. He was three months behind on his rent, and his store was about to be shuttered on him for good. He decided he'd play the lottery that night and if nothing happened he'd shoot himself. Since he also worked as a security guard, he had his revolver ready. That night his four numbers came up—and the amount he won was exactly enough, within a few cents, to pay his back rent. He was delighted, joyous, relieved—and also puzzled. For he wondered what this was telling him about the nature of the Universe he lived in, and what it might mean.

Just coincidence, right?

Or, as he said to me, should I be spending more time in church?

His situation raises some important questions. Does fate solve all our problems for us? Well, we know that isn't always true. So why does it solve some of them and not others? Answering these questions may mean we have to think in new ways about our experiences, and sometimes it means we'll have to visit an idea several times before it lets us feel its meaning.

Kurt Vonnegut, a novelist who deals elegantly with life's strange outcomes, puts it beautifully when he has an eccentric and hilarious character in his novel *Bluebeard* reflect on the strange coincidences in his life—only to deny them any validity.

> One would go mad if one took such coincidences too seriously.
> One might be led to suspect that there were all sorts of things going
> on in the Universe which he or she did not thoroughly understand. [1]

We always have the option of pretending there's nothing going on, after all.

I could add to this the curious instance of a short story I wrote in my twenties, an imaginative piece set in the future. I found it in my papers years later and I discovered, to my surprise, that the events described had come substantially true. I probably wouldn't have paid much attention to it but for the fact that some of the writers I have worked with over the years have reported, from time to time, the same sort of experience.

In these pages I'll be moving beyond these merely anecdotal stories of good luck and coincidence and suggesting that when we look at such events on their own they are hard to understand, but that often we can trace an underlying pattern. And it is the pattern of small and large nudges we get from chance and luck and fate that we may need to pay attention to. If we become conscious of what is happening to us we'll see such gifts everywhere and realize that synchronicity is beckoning to us. And once we see it, we may have to respond to its call.

What we'll find may surprise us, so I'll spell it out now. We'll see that to get into the flow of synchronicity we need to do three things:

- Trust that there is an energy in the universe that exists, and that it has a plan to use us to benefit our world. That trust has to be a deep trust.
- Be prepared to notice when this energy gives us help, and be alert to the many ways it can operate. If we're unaware of its methods we may stop noticing how

it comes into our lives. If we're ignorant we can't work with what arrives in terms of opportunity. Plenty of people are waiting for their "big break." It's a waste of time. The big break only ever happens because there were a lot of little breaks first—ones that someone worked at with plenty of energy and trust.

- Expect to be used by this synchronous energy in ways that seem not to be logical. The Universe has a plan, and we must learn to roll with it and do our part. So we have to let go of ego expectations and rewards. There *will* be rewards, but they probably won't be what we imagine... they'll be better. So don't set your heart on being an astronaut and be stubborn about it as a *goal*. Instead, set your heart's *intention*, then listen, pay attention, and see if that actually meshes with what the world sends you. If you're color-blind, NASA won't take you, no matter how much you may wish for it. But there will be another opening that is perfect for you—*if* you pay attention.

Deepak Chopra described this eloquently in an interview with Jean Houston. In the Vedanta, he explains, synchronicity is the condition of *Ritambharapragya*, and it has three elements:

> *Ritam* is the word for rhythm, order of the Universe;
> *Bhara* means "full of";
> *Pragya* means "mind."
> So, he whose mind, or she whose mind, is saturated with the rhythm of the cosmos. So when the elements and forces in you, and the elements and forces in the cosmos are totally aligned, then in that expression, in that field of almost choiceless awareness, a little subtle intention orchestrates its own fulfillment. [2]

Getting into this place—the space of synchronicity—is not as simple as wishing for something and then expecting it to appear. It involves aligning with the energies of the cosmos. We'll be looking at how we can do that.

Things That Get In Our Way

Yes, there will be things that prevent us from accepting synchronicity into our lives, and we'll have to take a good look at them in the second part of the book. This is important because if we know what traps our minds can set for us then we can avoid them more easily. It also has a more positive slant than just avoidance. When we see the errors we all can fall into, every one of us, we have the opportunity to grow our compassion. Our errors are not different from anyone else's. Seeing our own anger, for example, can lead us to think again about whether anger is even necessary. Usually it isn't.

Thinking in this way will inevitably cause us to have compassion for others' anger. Similarly, noticing our own greed and longing can make us more open and generous to those who are in the grip of greed and desire. Witnessing how we dislike others can lead us back to love and to loving those who are stuck in the place of hatred. We forgive them, and at the same time we forgive ourselves. Then we can let go of those negative feelings. Getting free of all these ego demands is what we need to do if we are to welcome synchronicity fully into our lives.

The Shadow

If you've ever found yourself feeling unexpectedly angry, or sad, or lost, this is almost certainly an upsurge of emotion that comes from the Unconscious, from the Shadow part of you—the part of you that perhaps you'd prefer not to acknowledge. If we are really to get free enough to follow where synchronicity leads us, we will have to make the descent into the self and meet what Carl Jung called the Shadow Self.

If we don't take steps to meet the Shadow Self, we cannot draw from its energy; instead we will fight it, exhausting ourselves. Think of it this way. If you have a terrifying dream, you can pretend it didn't happen, but if it comes back again and again this may not be possible. If you still try to ignore it, you may well find you're afraid to go to sleep at all, and that will soon ravage your health and happiness. Even sleeping tablets and alcohol won't work after awhile. The dream, and the unconscious material it holds, has to be faced, acknowledged, and worked through, or peace cannot be reestablished. Only then can you become authentically who you are. This is the Shadow talking to you. It lets you know it's there through dreams—and it also makes its presence felt when you move into a destructive, critical, or self-destructive frame of mind.

We can do this work before it becomes problematic, of course, and I'll be giving you the necessary guidance in these pages to make this possible. And if this sounds frightening, don't worry. We all have to meet the Shadow at some point in our lives, and we'll find it's more than ready to make friends with us, give us its gifts, and help us move forward. But we still have to meet it.

CHAPTER 2

The Guiding Hand

Synchronicity, Fate, and Your Future

In order to begin, paradoxically, we'll need to take a few steps back and start with some specific examples of society's prevailing attitudes to synchronicity, since they can shape our notions powerfully.

Here's one: "Comes the hour, comes the man." It's an old saying. It's rather reassuring, because it suggests that the right leader and inspirational thinker will emerge spontaneously at exactly the right moment, without any effort on our behalf. How lovely. Thinking like that could get us into a lot of trouble.

A better way to reformulate the idea might be to recognize that the right people will come forward at the precise moment they are needed only if we are already active in making sure we have a suitable pool of candidates, alert to what is likely to happen. That means we have to be cooperators with fate, not just passively acquiescent.

A more useful way to think about it can be found in the old Hindu saying, "When the student is ready the master appears." That's a rather different approach—one that also demands that we are participants in the process of personal growth.

This isn't just a personal choice. It's obvious that we will need good and alert people to help guide us through the changes ahead—it would be naïve to pretend that on a planet with energy crises, pollution problems, overpopulation, and nuclear proliferation that there will be no great challenges for us to face. The question is rather, how can we work with the unfolding future so that we can be sure it gives us the best possible outcome? How can we find our own place so that we are able to move into harmony with our own purpose and destiny?

What we'll see is that when we move out of the insular ego space of "my country," "my culture," "my corner of the world," and "my backyard," then we can move into the heart-space that tells us we are all connected, and there can only be solutions based on that awareness and that respect. Once in the heart-space, a new relationship with the future is possible—one that we co-create. When we allow ourselves to get to this place, then huge changes, miraculous changes, can occur. No, we probably can't stop the tides or the way the world spins on its axis, but we can change the way we are in the world. And at that point fate, destiny, or something we have no name for has an eerie habit of lending a hand.

We know this from personal experience. When we choose to "follow our bliss" (to use mythologist Joseph Campbell's famous phrase), what we do may not always be easy, and it may even feel impossibly hard at times, but we know that the hand of fate will often reach out and give us some help at particularly delicate moments.

Carl Jung, who pioneered the use of the word synchronicity in the way we're considering it here, felt that this was exactly what happened, although some of his followers prefer to say that synchronicity is a frame of mind only. To them it is the sort of situation when we start noticing specific events because we're suddenly sensitized to them.

An example might be that if we've been talking about dogs, we suddenly start noticing all the dogs that seem to pop up in our daily lives. The contention is that those dogs had always been there, but we just started noticing them. The effect is, for some people, to think the dogs have magically appeared. There's logic to this sort of analysis; and yet most of us are also only too well aware that this is not the whole of the equation—something bigger seems to be at issue.

Arthur Schopenhauer, the philosopher, was puzzled by this as well, and his essay "Transcendent Speculation on the Apparent Deliberateness in the Fate of the Individual" reflects this in its title.[1] He asks why it is that, looking back over one's life from the vantage point of old age, there so often seems to be a pattern to it that we could not discern at the time? He sees this and suggests that we create this pattern by using our unconscious will. Yet, we sense that there's a much bigger question at issue than he knows how to prove. Why couldn't we see this pattern earlier? And how would it have changed things if we had? And how does this unconscious will operate?

Most people don't talk about this deeper level much—about those miraculous coincidences, or about opportunities that have suddenly opened up for them. Perhaps it's a sense of embarrassment at seeming to boast about their good luck that stops them from shouting about it. Yet, I'd have to say that this idea is alive in our popular culture to a degree that is surprising, and in some unexpected places. It's something we are reluctant to acknowledge, but which we all know about.

We have only to think of the many Hollywood movies, widely enjoyed and deeply loved, that hinge on the idea that when we are doing what we truly love, something that feels authentic to us, then miracles or inspirations come to help us. Think of *The Natural, Field of Dreams, Forrest Gump, Slum Dog Millionaire,* or any of your favorite movies. Then think of the coincidences, the twists of fate, the strange circumstances that move the characters to where they need to be for the story to resolve itself. We could dismiss this, and say it's just plot manipulation by the writers to give us what we want. And that would be true. Hollywood knows how to make money off us. Or we could also say that we, the audiences, millions and millions of us, willingly accept this because it feels *right*. It corresponds to an inner reality that we already know about—even if we may not choose to believe it quite as strongly after we get out of the movie. That inner reality is about how fate and destiny will cooperate with us when we are on the authentic path of the heart.

Perhaps that's why the greatest literature of the past three millennia or so has returned to this topic so often. Perhaps this is because it feels true to us, in our hearts, even though it seems counterintuitive.

Popular legends from all times and ages echo this, even if they are not "literature," *per se,* but folk tales. The probably apocryphal story of Robert the Bruce, the Scots king who fought against the English, is a case in point. It has had an enduring charm for generations.

In the story, Robert the Bruce has lost yet another battle and is sitting in a cave trying to work out what went wrong. As he sits there, exhausted and depressed, he watches a spider crawl up its web. He brushes it aside. After all, he's a king, and even kings on the run don't put up with spiders. The next thing he knows the spider is back in the same place, still trying to make a web. He again brushes it aside and continues brooding. When he looks up some time later the spider is back again, laboring to create a web. Robert pauses. Suddenly he gets the message: never give up. Inspired, he goes back to campaigning and, as we know from history, frees Scotland from British domination. This could not have happened if he hadn't been alert and listening to what the Universe was telling him. Perhaps the real lesson is twofold: never give up, and listen for the messages the Universe is sending you. [2]

Robert the Bruce died in A.D.1329. What's interesting is that this tale is echoed by another from the far side of the world, which tells of the great ruler Tamerlane of Persia watching an ant climbing a grass stalk. It is in essence exactly the same tale. Tamerlane was born in A.D.1336, so the time period is very similar, too. [3]

An even older tale also covers the same theme. King Alfred of England, who died in A.D. 899, found himself in a similar situation. He, too, can't seem to win his battles against the marauding Danes, and he's on the run, dejected, sitting in a hut, and he's been told to make sure the coarse oatcakes on the griddle don't burn. We can already see a resemblance here to the other two tales, I'm sure. Well, Alfred spends so much energy brooding that, of course, the cakes burn, and there's nothing for anyone to eat that night. The peasant woman who has given him shelter comes back and yells at him for spoiling their food. And at that point Alfred recognizes that he has a duty to make sure his people are fed and able to exist in peace. He gathers his wits and is inspired to renew a struggle that ultimately sees the Danish raiders brought under control. In England, King Alfred is still known as "Alfred the Great," even though he was not the most powerful king of his era. Such is the respect he inspires that he is one of the few kings from that murky time period that almost every English person can identify. [4]

It really doesn't matter if the tales are factually true or not; what matters is that they have articulated something that feels psychologically and spiritually true. This is quite simply that for those who are on a path of getting free (whether it be free of oppression, so that they can become who they need to be, or free of other ties), even the depths of defeat can provide inspiration. All we have to do is remain open to it. And above all we must not give in to despair, self-pity, or become passive. We are *expected* to be co-creators of the future.

At their center, all three stories have distant echoes in them of the Jesus story. The moment of defeat, the crucifixion, turned out to be the moment of greatest victory. The crosses and crucifixes in churches everywhere are the symbols of that transformation. What they tell us is that when we face defeat we may, in fact, be only just reaching the turning point that leads to victory. We descend to the darkest part of the self so that we can regain the energy that is there.

The mythic structure is essentially the same for all these stories. Behind that the main lesson is as we have already noticed: trust totally that you have a purpose, be alert to what comes, and work with what arrives.

In each tale the student was ready, and the teacher *did* appear—even if it was only a spider, or an ant, or a peasant woman shouting angrily about her burned food.

CHAPTER 3

Head Versus Heart

Flow and Force:
Getting Your Freedom Back

At least two types of energy exist in our bodies at any one time. The first is the energy of the brain, of what we tend to call the mind. It can do complex calculations of all kinds; it can even fill in government forms. It is, therefore, a very superior energy, and no one denies it exists. The second is the energy of the heart. The heart is not merely a pump that circulates the blood; the heart is a powerful organ with a discernable electromagnetic field that is measurably more powerful than the one the brain produces.[1] We all know there are some things that, in popular speech, we think of as coming from the brain, and there are other things that we feel come from the heart. Sometimes the two clash.

This split between head and heart is one of the major problems we face as human beings. The head has come to dominate our culture, as people rush to take advantage of each other, to amass wealth, and to collect things that provide solace for the ego. In the process they often leave the heart bereft—they have gained the whole world but lost their souls.

If we are to be fulfilled as humans, we may have to reverse this accepted orthodoxy that places the brain in control of everything, because it clearly does not always work for our long-term happiness. We may have to put the heart impulses first and the head impulses in auxiliary mode, helping us to find our true heart-selves. For when we are in the heart-space we can find our way to being in tune with a powerful energy in the Universe. I'll call it being "in the flow," but we could just as easily call it something else. Being in the flow requires us to work in harmony with destiny; it is an aspect of synchronicity. When we are in the flow—when we allow the Universe to use us for its own ends rather than self-aggrandizement—then we move in tune with destiny.

Flow and Force

Contrasting with the idea of flow is another term, which I call "force." When we force things in life we insist that our way is the only way, and we do not allow any space for things to be otherwise. We don't allow space for the happy accident or the fortunate discovery. It's our way that takes precedence. When we do this the ego is in charge, and often the ego cannot see clearly enough what is needed, so the mission goes awry.

When we allow for flow, something entirely different happens. We leave space for the accidental. We listen for what is happening. Artists of all kinds do this when they start a drawing or a poem or a song and find that something that just happened along is exactly right. That smudge in the corner might be just what's needed. The sound of the dog barking outside turns out to be perfect for the recording, or perhaps leads the artist into an entirely new and productive direction. This is "flow" as I'm using the term here.

Flow allows us to welcome the unusual, and not to reject something just because it doesn't fit our preconceived notions. With preconceived notions we close our eyes to possibility. We say, in effect, that we don't want what fate, or God, or the Universe, provides. Sometimes, when I've been working on a project I've had to remind myself to accept, and not reject. I have to remind myself to try less hard, rather than forcing ahead. Or perhaps someone comes into my life, and I may say, "I don't have time for this person right now." I can ignore this person easily if I just close off my heart. Or I can listen—and perhaps that person inspires me, and introduces me to someone else who inspires me farther. Things happen that I could never have predicted. If we accept this as the Hand of God, why refuse what it offers? After all, God knows lots more people than we do. Staying open is part of being in the flow, even if it looks at times like there's no discernable direction. But the river knows where it is going. So don't fight the river. Make friends with it. Use its energy for what you need.

Getting in the flow is not something that we have to learn; it is instead something that requires us to un-learn certain rather persistent habits of mind. These habits include worry, obsessing over details, and second-guessing ourselves. These are all things that get in our way, and they all come from the ego. They are things we do every day when we attempt to control the outcomes of what we do. Perhaps at such times we should remember Krishna's advice to Arjuna in the sacred text the *Bhagavad Gita*: "Act selflessly, without any thought of personal profit." [2]

Consider an athlete at a sporting event. Ideally, this athlete focuses on feeling right, not on how she looks or who is in the crowd, or what she's going to tell her colleagues at work the next day. And when she runs that race, or skis that winning course, or whatever it is she is about to do, if she's doing it well she'll be in a space that has very little to do with everyday worries. When those worries intrude she will lose her sense of being fully in the activity, and she'll almost certainly not do as well. This is the way flow works. Whether she wins the gold medal or just places well matters far less than that she is, for the time she's doing the event, at one with it. Then she'll be doing her best.

We know this to be true. Some of us may have been fortunate enough to experience it, and it's a feeling unlike most of our other workaday feelings. How would our lives be if we were simply to stay in that space?

Unfortunately for us, we live in a world that values this flow experience only when it is seen in certain circumstances, such as in sports. The rest of the time we're expected to pay rent, make sure our bills are paid on time, and so on. There is, therefore, a balance we have to work out between the practicalities of the everyday world and our ability to go toward the flow. If we get it wrong, if we veer too far one way rather than another, then we are seen as eccentric or even as dangerous failures. The person who chooses to be in the flow of painting large canvasses all day, while the children run barefoot in the rain, is likely soon to have the department of social services on the doorstep. Joseph Campbell put it beautifully in an interview when he said that it was a knife edge and not getting it right was actively dangerous. "They crucified Jesus for it," [3] he said. Jesus chose to live in the world of spiritual truth, and that upset the political powers of the time.

South African Archbishop Desmond Tutu, when asked how he managed to stay in the world of the spirit and yet still be in the realm of international political negotiation, said that he found it almost impossible *not* to be in the realm of the spirit. Obviously, he's a man who has helped to bring about great changes, and he has also excited some serious antipathy from powerful people in the process. [4]

Make no mistake: there are destructive forces out there that don't really want us to live in the flow. All of these forces come from the ego mind-set of ourselves and others. They'll allow us to be in the flow only under certain circumstances, and the rest of the time they'd prefer us to be doing something more down-to-earth. Those powerful forces will manifest as repressive governments and their agencies in certain parts of the world. But let us also be aware that at times these forces may include your friends, your parents, and even your children, as well as the things you tell yourself about who you are. Your own history may work against you, too, because you may not believe you can stay in the place of flow.

So let's not have any conspiracy theories trying to assign blame where it doesn't belong. *This is something we do to ourselves.* We're surrounded by those we love, and who love us, and perhaps they're telling us not to be a concert pianist but to take the good safe job at an electronic video-simulated keyboard factory. It's pretty hard to resist. The reasons they give us for not following our preferred activity are all good ones. They all make perfect sense. And so most of us confine the areas in which we truly flow to hobbies or "recreation activities."

In this book, we are going to take a close look at the ways in which we talk ourselves out of the experience of flow and the empowerment that comes with it. I choose to focus on you, the individual, because the task is always personal. We each have to free ourselves first, then stay free. Driving a bulldozer through a prison wall will let the inmates out, but if they are still intent on a life of crime it won't be long before they're back behind bars. We need to free ourselves first, and that means getting free of those habits of mind that wind up confining us. This is a necessary step toward living with synchronicity.

Getting Your Freedom Back

Getting our freedom back is not always easy, and there's no guarantee that it will be materially rewarding or profitable. Very often it doesn't look profitable at all in conventional terms. And yet I've taught classes for more than 20 years in which writers have announced that they were going to give up their day jobs and become poets, bassists in rock bands, painters, mountain climbers, installation artists, actors, and so on. They've done it, too, and taken on all the attendant hardships cheerfully—flow has meant that much to them. Why? Well, when they are in this space, these artists (for they are all artists of some kind at this point) say that they feel the energy of the Universe working through them. They may say it in a variety of ways, but the underlying reason is always that they sense that something bigger than themselves is showing them what to do. No wonder they can't go back to the everyday world without a struggle!

My fellow teachers are varied in the topics they teach, but in speaking with them I can see that they, too, are united in their intention of moving their students closer to being in this flow. I'm thinking of a sculptor and visual artist whose drawing classes have opened countless hundreds of eyes and minds and inspired people to bring more creativity into their lives. I'd point to an inspired yoga teacher who does the same thing by asking people to observe the way they feel about their bodies as they practice yoga. And I'm thinking of a teacher of drawing who is, in fact, someone who helps others reclaim their creative selves.

I try to do the same thing in my classes and workshops because I understand the feeling of being in the flow—and what happens when we lose it. When we are fortunate enough to have flow magically arise in our lives, we have to honor it.

I joke to my friends and students that I've given up writing more often than anybody I know. I've been frustrated, angry, deliriously happy, disappointed, and morose. I've sworn that I'll never write another word because it all takes too much time and pain and effort. Yet I keep coming back to it, because when I'm in the flow, when I feel the words coming, no matter what else is going on in my life, then I feel myself to be the servant of something that needs to be acknowledged.

Eric Maisel, the gifted writer and therapist, puts it in a way I truly enjoy. [5] He points out that for creative people not creating becomes so unbearable that eventually they give in and start creating again, sometimes complaining all the way that it doesn't pay, that a nine-to-five job pays better on a per-hour basis. And so on. You can almost hear the dialogue of the head—*It doesn't pay!*—as it wrestles unsuccessfully with the heart—*I love doing this anyway* . . . The point is that we are all creative people; it's just that some of us don't know it yet.

Andrew Cohen, the writer and mystic, puts it this way; he says that the Universe doesn't have arms and legs and hands, but we do. [6] Our job, therefore, is to express what the Universe wants expressed, since we are the only creatures who can do that. Our task is to serve the Universe this way.

Whether you see that as literal truth or as an elegant metaphor for the creative process is up to you. And perhaps in the end it doesn't much matter which interpretation we place on it. The point is that when we allow ourselves to be in this creative flow we—all of us—become more humane, more compassionate, less ego-filled, and more loving. We are rendered simultaneously more humble because we feel the power of what is happening, and we are inspired, knowing we are part of this. We are following our hearts, and we know it's the right thing to do. Nothing else comes close. And as we do so the Universe has a way of cooperating with us, sending us inspirations, opportunities, and life-enhancing experiences we could not have received if we'd stayed home pursuing a safe and steady job. That is the experience of synchronicity.

Now this may make the whole discussion sound very ponderous, so I'll add an anecdote told about the nineteenth century Indian saint Ramakrishna. He had been telling those who came to speak with him to follow what they loved, and a woman asked to see him one day. She said she was having a hard time with this because there was nothing she loved. "Nothing?" asked the sage. "Nothing," she replied. "Really?" he asked again. She thought for a bit, then said that actually she did love something—she loved her little nephew. Well then, said Ramakrishna, there is your answer.

Like the woman in the anecdote, we may already be in a heart-space, but we discount it, or fail to value it, so to all intents and purposes it's not there, and so we can't get into the flow of energy it provides. Our task is to see how we can get more flow into our lives, and be more in touch with synchronicity, more of the time, while also making sure the rent gets paid and our children don't go barefoot.

CHAPTER 4

Practical Examples of Flow and Synchronicity from Real Life

Let me show you what I mean about synchronous events by giving you some examples. I'm sure some of you will resonate with some of these, since we've all had days when things have gone miraculously, or strangely, our way. Patti Smith, the poet and singer, describes this sort of event beautifully when she writes about her band coming together in New York City and playing in a scruffy pool hall:

> As the band played on, you could hear the whack of the pool cue hitting the balls, the saluki [a type of dog] barking, bottles clinking, the sounds of a scene emerging. Though no one knew it, the stars were aligning, the angels were calling. [1]

It's sometimes only afterward that we realize that something momentous just was set in motion. So, here's a personal anecdote that may help.

When I first came to live in the United States in 1986, I had no job, and for a while I painted walls, tutored kids, and picked up whatever work I could here and there. Even though I had some fun, I wasn't actually using my Oxford doctorate nor my counseling skills. I knew I was just trying to get by and that I wasn't fully engaged in what I was doing. I was on the verge of taking a job with a rehabilitation center for teenagers, which required long hours, paid poorly, and which I knew from experience could be heart-breaking work. Then I saw an advertisement for a teaching job at a local college. Teaching was something I knew I was competent at doing. I wrote off and was called for an interview.

The day of the interview I brushed off my only suit, tidied myself up, and took my map. I had no car, but I knew where the college was, if not the details of how to get there. Still, I reckoned it couldn't be too difficult to find if hundreds of students managed it each day. So I took the subway to the end of the line and figured that I'd find a cab or a bus and that would be simple. Coming from England, where there were cabs and buses almost everywhere, I had no fears. Still, I left a good chunk of time because I hate to be late. I got off the subway and found myself in what was then a very seedy area of town. Lots of people were about, all were black, and quite a few didn't understand English. Or perhaps it was just my English they couldn't understand.

There were no cabs in sight, and the bus went exactly twice a day, I was told, if I cared to wait until 6 p.m. So I found a phone and called a cab company. No one wanted to come and pick me up. I couldn't believe it. I tried again. No pickups in that area. I looked around. The place didn't look dangerous. In fact, it looked pretty neat to me, with plenty of cool ethnic shops displaying colorful items I wished I had time to look at; but the cab companies, all of them, seemed to disagree.

So I asked the way from a friendly passerby and decided I'd walk. Time was ticking away fast now. Just to be on the safe side, I decided to start walking and hold out my hitch-hiking thumb as well. Even in an urban area it might just be possible to find a lift, I thought, since I'd hitch-hiked all over Europe as a kid.

The day was fine, I was walking along, best suit, briefcase, umbrella, and one hand held out, thumb extended, when a car screeched to a halt beside me. It was rather dramatic. Inside was a decidedly beautiful young woman, a whole carful of groceries in brown bags, and a baby. "Get in" she said. By now, other cars were honking at her for blocking the road. So I got in and held the baby on my lap.

"You looked a bit desperate," she said. I explained that I was trying to get to a job interview at the college, whereupon she looked over and said, "Well, you're going in completely the wrong direction." Then, just as I was about to volunteer to get out she said, "What the heck. I'll take you there," and pulled a U-turn so tight that I was temporarily smothered in grocery bags.

"When do you have to be there?" she yelled over the rising volume of a none-too-perfect exhaust system, and when I said in about 10 minutes she muttered something and stamped on the gas. Her large, far-from-new car didn't exactly fly, but I do recall a light that had just turned red and was just as promptly ignored. I made cooing sounds to the baby and thanked the auburn-haired damsel for her kindness. I felt that if I had to be rescued, then a beautiful woman in an aging sedan was a wonderful variation on the theme.

We arrived at the college gates. I handed back the baby and was thanking her until she cut me short—"You'll be late," she said, "you'd better get a move on."

I trotted up to the security shed at the main gate and asked about the place I was supposed to go for an interview. The guard was not helpful. Who was I? Why did I have to be there? And no, he didn't have a map of the campus.

As we were talking, a huge green Lincoln Continental pulled up. I know it was a Lincoln because at that point it was one of the few American cars I could actually recognize, and chiefly because of its size. The person at the wheel turned out to be the director of one of the college departments, and he kindly drove me half a mile, right to the door of the building I needed. Since it had no sign on it I would never have been able to identify it on my own, especially as the campus was in vacation mode at that time and there was no one around to ask.

I ran up the stairs three at a time to the place my interview was to be. I looked at my watch. I was exactly one minute and 30 seconds late. That could be enough to create a bad impression. Fortunately, the previous candidate was still in the room, so I had a second or two to catch breath.

Do you see how unlikely this tale must sound?

By the time I was called in for the interview I felt that I'd already had a very odd kind of day, and I wasn't nervous at all. I was simply myself. Then one of the interviewers asked me a question that was supposed to test some aspect of my teaching ability. He said, "What would you do if you came to class one day and half the students were not there, and the other half didn't want to be there?" The way he phrased the question suggested he doubted I'd know what to do under such a circumstance. I could see it in his eyes; and perhaps he wanted to show me up as somehow deficient. My reply said itself before I even knew it. "Well," I said, "you can't do much about people who aren't there . . ." The whole panel of interviewers erupted in laughter. We spent the next hour having a great, wide-ranging conversation, and I got the job.

Looking back over those events now it seems almost impossible that they should have turned out as they did. Had I taken the cab ride I'd probably have arrived tense, defensive, and determined to "do my best." Instead, I arrived a bit tousled and in a different mind-space, and that allowed me just to be myself.

I've now been in that job for 25 years. It hasn't always been perfect, and I've made lots of mistakes over the years, but they were mostly to do with me, not the job itself. They were all times when I tried to force things along. And now, looking back over it all, I can say with some assurance that the job was exactly what I needed, given who I was at the time. It gave me scope and energy and set me on a path that has led to me typing these words. Surely I've had my doubts and miseries at times—who doesn't? But I have no doubt this was the right thing for me at that time.

It wasn't what I wanted—in my vanity I wanted something more illustrious. But I have to say it was exactly what I needed for my personal growth. There's a major difference between "want" and "need." Circumstances had placed me exactly where I needed to be.

So what does this mean? Does it mean I had a guardian angel guiding me that day? Perhaps. Does it mean I was incredibly lucky? Yes, I can only agree with that. Could one say that the guiding hand of fate was at work? We could certainly say so.

Carl Jung would have put it differently. He suggested that when we are on a path that has to do with what is most authentic within us, then we tap into the energies of the Collective Unconscious, the deep wisdom that exists in the human race and which guides us—if we let it. If we stop being purely rational and instead decide to follow intuitions and inspirations, Jung claimed, these powers will surface to guide us.

In his personal journal, the *Red Book*, he ascribes the power of foreseeing the future to this level of awareness. He refused to publish the *Red Book* (it appeared only in 2009, 40 years after his death) because he was afraid of what his colleagues would say about his mystical ideas. I mention this merely because when we start talking about these kinds of topics there is inevitably an upsurge of resistance from people who don't believe it could be anything other than coincidence. Jung, by contrast, felt that what we call coincidences were evidence of synchronicities—moments when the energy of the Universe works to show us the way ahead.

I do not intend to engage in an argument here as to whether or not these events happen because of God, the Universe, or pure chance. They do happen. I bet you're reading this and saying, yes, I've had a few moments like that, too. Don't discount them. Consider them as moments when you, for whatever reasons, were in the flow of life. You can even try asking your friends if they've ever had moments like this— and what you hear may surprise you.

I'll add another personal example here. When I met the woman who was to become my second wife, I was at a party given by some friends and was getting ready to leave because it had been a long day for me. When Cat walked in I knew I had to introduce myself to her—I've no idea why. I could see she was very attractive, but I was aware of something more than that. I recall saying to myself that I wanted to know her, of all the people in the room.

We began talking. Perhaps because I was already tired I was able to relax enough just to be me (have you noticed that was a component of the previous story?). When she mentioned she was divorced with two children I was surprised. She looked so young. I had already been divorced, without children. So when Cat mentioned her children my immediate response was, "Oh, I'd like to meet them." Since I'd only just met her this seemed like a huge liberty to take. She might have thought I was a child molester, or just plain pushy, or worse. In fact, the moment I said it I knew it was exactly the right thing to have said.

To this day I've no clear idea why I said it. I could have said something neutral like, "Tell me more about your children," or something even less definite. But I didn't. The words rose to my lips because I knew I really did want to meet these children, but most of all I knew I wanted to be part of the life of this family. That was 20 years ago, and I could not have imagined a better partner for my life, nor I for hers.

If you ask Cat for her side of the story, she'd agree with all this, and she'd add that she visualized me about two weeks before we met. She decided that what she needed was someone just like me. And suddenly there I was.

I mention this in such detail not because I want to show off my life. I mention it simply because personal experiences like this are powerful, and when we start to ask around we'll find there are plenty of other examples in other lives. I hope that perhaps you are, right now, making connections with events in your life that seemed as if they were inevitable or even fated.

My late colleague, the opera singer Bill Flavin, recalled that on the first date he had with his beloved Corinne they had tea together, and as they were walking along Boylston Street in Boston she started humming something. Bill listened. After all they were both musicians. Corinne was a cellist for the Boston Symphony Orchestra. He turned to Corinne and asked her if she knew what she was humming. No, she replied, it was just something that had come to her. She was humming Mendelssohn's "Wedding March."

Bill tells me he proposed on the spot. Corinne was taken aback, but she agreed to think about it, and their harmonious marriage lasted until she died, some 48 years later. What was that moment of knowing? Where did it come from? And was it just luck that allowed them to make their marriage work, or was there some real connection, even on that first date, that was telling them to pay attention?

Whatever we want to call it, I'd like us to consider it as "flow," as what happens when we get out of our heads and start listening with our whole being. When we are in such a space we know we're doing what is right for us, no matter what others may say, and no matter how odd it may seem. This is not the same as impulsiveness. This comes from somewhere deeper, more vital.

And let's be clear about another thing. Being in the flow is not about being passive. We have to go out there and do our part, or nothing can happen. Expecting the Universe to do everything for you is about as reasonable as expecting it to place food in your mouth and then chew it for you, too. Every baby knows that she has to suck the nipple that is presented to her, and learn how to feed and how to be fed. It's perhaps the second great lesson we learn, the first being that we have to breathe the air by gulping it in first. Both lessons are the same: learn to cooperate with the world, work with it, or you'll soon die.

Now, if we return to the story of how I met Cat, we could, each of us, have imagined a very wealthy future spouse, well connected, who would make our professional lives easy. We could have asked the Universe to do all the hard work for us and just hand us a gift. I don't think it would have cooperated. What Cat and I did, individually, was to ask the divine energies that run the Universe for a vital and loving relationship that would help each of us grow—and that is what we got. It took some courage on both our parts to see the situation that turned up as exactly what we needed. Either of us could have walked away. But we didn't.

So what can we say about all this? The sequence here seems to be:

1. Ask for what you need (not what you would like);
2. Pay attention to what arrives;
3. Act with courage;
4. Be prepared to work hard with whatever situation comes.

We'll be dealing with each of these in the chapters that follow.

Learning these lessons we realize we are co-creative with the world. The Universe gives us opportunities and we have to deal with them as best we can. When we see this, we cannot help but realize that this is the nature of fate and destiny. We are humans, we will die—and between now and then we get to choose how we live our lives. Since we can't know with any certainty when we will die, or whom we will marry, or how many children we might or might not have, the making of plans is always going to be a tenuous adventure. Living usually requires us to let go of our version of how things ought to be in order to accommodate how they actually are. So we have to learn to love and accept that. We have to learn to be in tune with fate and accept the guiding hand it extends. In accepting flow we move toward living synchronous lives.

CHAPTER 5

Ask For What You Need

I'm going to spell out what being in tune with fate and accepting the hand it extends means because it is often the single most difficult concept for most people to understand.

Many people cannot tell the difference between what they'd like in their fantasies and what they actually need—which may be very different. I may wish to be famous, but what I might need, for the growth of my soul, is some hard work that tests my faith and helps me to become stronger.

Now, imagine a person who decides to ask for a million dollars and a new car. When I do workshop exercises centered on this topic, many people ask for something very similar to the above. And who wouldn't like that? We can't blame the desire. But we must be careful here, for the Universe has a tendency to give us exactly what we ask for, except not, perhaps, in the precise way we had imagined.

If we analyze this particular wish, what we are very likely to find is a person who wants the money and the car for a reason, usually a selfish reason. One young man put it beautifully when he said that the money would mean he wouldn't have to struggle at a useless job, since he had no idea what he wanted to do with his life, and the car would allow him to show his friends he'd "hit the big time." He wanted a shortcut to personal confidence.

But what his request was actually saying was, "I'm worried about my status, I'm confused about my purpose in life, I'm insecure, and that's where I spend a lot of time and energy." The Universe isn't going to hear the request he sent about the car and the cash. Those are just words. The Universe is going to respond to his energy and emotions. It's going to see a man who is desperately unsure of himself—and it will give him more of the same.

What we focus on is what we get more of.

Another comparison may help here. My neighbor has a dog that barks a lot. This annoys him, and many other people. So when the dog barks, he yells at it. What message does the dog get? The dog gets the message that noise is fun and getting angry is good. Obviously it must be! He barks, his owner makes more noise, and he gets to bark more. What fun! And so every day the dog barks more, and more happily than before. Now, I love dogs dearly, and I even like this one. I also see it as a splendid example of how the Universe works. The Universe does not respond to our words so much as our emotions—how we say what we say.

The point that we have to establish, and learn to respect fully, is that we manifest at exactly the same level that our thoughts and emotions are capable of reaching. People all over the world are manifesting things they don't want, simply because they haven't cleared their minds and hearts sufficiently beforehand. Writer and mystic Alan Cohen puts this beautifully: "Everyone and everything that shows up in our life is a reflection of something that is happening inside of us." [1]

The gift that lies in this recognition is that we can regard everything that does turn up in our lives as a message that is instructive—everyone is our teacher, as the Buddha says—since we can learn most about ourselves from those who are difficult. That way we raise our awareness of what we are asking for, and can become conscious of ways we are thwarting ourselves. Here is Alan Cohen again: "Joy is not the result of getting what you want; it's the way to get what you want. In the deepest sense, it is what you want." [2]

The task before us, therefore, is not simple. We have to raise our emotional awareness so that we can manifest what we actually need. That means we have to recognize that there are no shortcuts, and that what we wish for today may be the best we can attain at the moment. Then, when things turn up, we must accept that we've had a part in bringing them to our door. As we grow we'll be able to choose better each time, and in this way we'll be able to be fully in the flow of synchronicity. This is our part of the arrangement, and it takes some effort and some faith.

One of the best things to consider is that when we ask for things, do we ask only for ourselves? For instance, do we want a bigger house simply because it will raise our status with our family and neighbors? If you ask for something only for yourself there's a good chance that the Universe will hear only that you're thinking about your status, and so will send you further things that cause you to fill your mind with doubts about your status. Try this: ask not just for yourself, but for the world.

This isn't simply a sleight of hand. If you truly do want a larger house, for example, ask yourself what you are going to do with that space. Is it just to show off? Or do you want it because you have a sense of how you could be a more effective parent/business person/contributor to society if you had that house? When synchronous events send you what you desire, are you going to use what arrives to take yourself to the next step?

Can you see the difference? Asking in this way has a purity of purpose and intent to it that focuses your request in a far more powerful way. Asking in a meaningful way is much more likely to produce results, and we need to know how to ask. In the process we'll also have to make sure we stay clear of a few traps. That's what we'll be examining in the pages that follow.

Some Definitions

Now is probably the time to wrestle with a few definitions—although I have to tell you that they may prove unsatisfactory, since we'll be attempting to be precise about some very slippery concepts. So far we've looked at synchronicity and the idea of flow as opposed to force. So how do these concepts tie in with other headline words, such as fate, destiny, the guiding hand, dharma, and karma?

Fate and destiny are words that have been used so loosely here in the West that it seems all but impossible to get them straight, although they both tell us that there is an ultimate goal that is, somehow, going to happen no matter what. "It was fated to happen" and "it's destined" are used interchangeably by most people.

So let's look at dharma and karma as alternate ways of framing the information that may help us out of the vagueness. In Hindu and Buddhist thought, karma is a law, not a possibility. Broadly speaking, karma means what goes around comes around. If I do something evil it will come back to me, and likewise if I do something good. If evil things happen to me then I must acknowledge the law and not perpetuate it by doing something evil back. I may be simply expiating karma from a previous incarnation.

Dharma, though, is a little less easily defined. In Hindu thought, dharma has to do with the attitude I bring to what I do. I can give money to charity, but if I do so grudgingly then I alter the harmony of my corner of the world, and ultimately that affects the whole of the larger world, even if only slightly. It is a version of free will, which allows me some freedom, although it also acknowledges the concept of divine law—I should want to do what is right, but I may still choose something else.

Dharma is, then, both the existence of harmony and the action of following the way toward harmony. We know we're on the dharma path because we feel the harmony we are moving in and with—in some ways this is synchronicity as we have described it. It is not about forcing but about being. [3]

What's useful about dharma and karma is that they can help us to see the ideas of fate and destiny a little more clearly. The eastern and western concepts are not that different, in essence, showing us that this is a universal discussion. All humanity has wrestled with this at some time over the past three millennia, at least, and the results have not been all that different. In each case there is a sense that events will unfold in a certain way, and that we have some choices in how we behave as they do so, and that our actions can affect the outcome. Those choices can lead to greater chaos or greater harmony—so ideally we will choose the route of greater harmony, if we can see it.

Obviously we could go into more detail, yet I feel that this is a good enough working definition for now, since we will have to stay open and flexible if we are to see how things work. The existence of these terms was, in my view, never intended to be specific, since human beings can't really be expected to be able to define something so much bigger than we are. The terms are, and always have been, approximate. The words allow us to talk about the concepts.

And that's why we need literature, so we can see the concepts in action.

CHAPTER 6

Synchronicity in Literature

Paying Attention to What
Comes Our Way

About now you're probably wondering about some objective evidence for the existence of flow and the guiding hand I'm talking of. I'm not sure it can be demonstrated scientifically, although there's plenty of evidence of an anecdotal sort that says it exists.

One specific clue exists in an obvious place, though. Almost all the great legends and most of the western world's great literature for the past two millennia hinges on this idea of doing what feels right rather than doing what we can calculate as being to our specific advantage. When we follow what feels right, events conspire to help us. Joseph Campbell made this point clear in his many lectures and books, when he said that the essence of the hero's journey—a major theme throughout literature—involved not taking the safe way but in following the internal promptings of the heart that might seem like a very unsafe way indeed.

One example of this is that when Sir Gawain goes on his pilgrimage to fight the Green Knight in the famous medieval legend, he thinks he is going to certain death. But he goes anyhow, because taking the "safe" route of running away would destroy his sense of honor. It would break his heart, he knows. Along the way he is helped by certain coincidences, and the Green Knight spares his life. When he returns with his mixed tale of success and failure he knows that fate has taken him where he needed to go so he could develop his wisdom.

Sir Gawain left on his journey with a rigid code of carefully defined moral behavior, but when he comes back he has a more compassionate and humble heart. And we could add many instances to this. Literature is not "true" in the sense of being factually accurate in every detail. It is, instead, a metaphor that describes certain vital internal spiritual processes. This is what we are talking about, now. Literature is filled with such metaphors, especially of the journey toward greater wisdom. In fact, it seems to be such a basic theme that we could argue that literature and legend reinforce the central idea: things happen for a reason.

> **EXERCISE:** One thing you can do, right now, is to identify three or four of the turning points of your own life. By this I mean times when you realized that something had changed for you, and that you didn't see the world quite the same way again. Jot them down right now. Take a few minutes. If you wish, you can write more about these events and why they feel important.

When I've done this exercise with various groups I've been astonished at what has come to light. A woman announced to a very surprised group that it wasn't until a bat flew into her bedroom, and she became frightened that she might have contracted rabies while shooing it out, that she realized how much she wanted to live. Until the bat arrived that dark and overcast night, she'd been planning, with some care, how she would kill herself. After the bat had gone, she knew she wanted to live and was now terrified that she'd die of rabies, since she'd been scratched and possibly bitten by it. A man in the same group recorded how a planned trip to Maine got derailed. He'd met the person he was to spend his life with, and they drove south to Massachusetts, instead, where they stayed for the next 40 years.

It's not until we take the time to see how strange and haphazard our lives seem to be that we realize that we, to a greater or lesser extent, have been following our hearts much of the time, and that when we do so there is a guiding hand that manages things for us.

Sometimes we can ignore the guiding hand, too. When I was a graduate student at Oxford, I accepted an invitation to give a talk to the local theatrical troupe in a neighboring town. There was no pay, and it would take time and effort, but I went along. After the talk, a woman asked me what I was studying, and I told her I was writing a thesis on Joseph Conrad. She looked thoughtful and said she should put me in touch with her friend who had some unpublished letters from Conrad. I followed up the lead, and was soon gazing at half a dozen of these unknown literary letters, each one a gem. I was immensely grateful and said so. I knew I could get a couple of periodical publications for my fledgling career out of this, at least. What a gift! My ego was very happy, I can tell you.

Of course, I was very grateful for this stroke of luck and gave each person a small present, which was about as far as my meager funds allowed. And that was when the man who had the letters said I should perhaps contact his uncle, as well. It turned out the uncle had 12 huge folio-sized albums of his grandfather's in which were some 50 more letters—from Conrad, Henry James, H. G. Wells, Thomas Hardy, and others. All the great literary figures of the age were represented. There was even a note from Charles Dickens. Eventually, I wrote 17 scholarly articles on these unpublished letters, and as a result of this windfall, which may have helped my career at that time, I gained a renewed sense of the strangeness of fate.

But there was more to come. Twenty years later, the publisher of the collected edition of Thomas Hardy's letters contacted me to ask if he could see the letters themselves and did I know who had them? In those 20 years, they seem to have disappeared entirely. The people I had talked to could not be traced. The documents may now be permanently lost. Perhaps at the time I thought my luck was serving me. Now I think with gratitude that I was the instrument that allowed these things not to be lost without a trace.

It wasn't until I was preparing those articles for publication (back in 1984) that I remembered something else. About two years earlier, through a string of circumstances, I had wound up traveling to Cambridge and talking about my studies with a complete stranger. This man, I now recalled, had also said he thought he knew where some other Conrad letters might be. I hadn't written down the details, and at the time I wasn't particularly interested in that scholarly direction—I was only interested in getting to Cambridge to see why the girl I loved wasn't responding the way I hoped, and I was mostly concerned to try and work out how I could get her to see things differently. In the process, I ignored what fate was sending me. In fact, I'd dropped the ball so thoroughly I didn't even remember dropping it until much later. I was trying to force things in one direction when they clearly wanted me to go in another.

If you've experienced something like this, take a moment now, to write it down. Sometimes we insist on not seeing what we are meant to see, because we're not paying attention to what arrives. But when we're ready, the stars align and the angels sing.

CHAPTER 7

Act with Courage

The Metaphor of Prince
Five Weapons

So, how do we raise our personal awareness in order to ask the Universe for what we need? How can we help ourselves toward the flow of synchronicity? Fortunately, we have several myths to instruct us as to what we can expect. Let's look at a couple.

For example, one story told of the Buddha was that, two incarnations before he became the Buddha, he was Prince Five Weapons facing the monster Sticky Hair.

In the story, Prince Five Weapons has just left his weapons master, fully trained, and is feeling pretty good about himself, when he's confronted by the monster Sticky Hair blocking his path and threatening him. The prince shoots his arrows at the monster, but the arrows merely stick in the monster's hair. He then tries his sword. Same result. Then he hurls his spear, and the same thing happens. Next he tries his club. It, too, sticks. Finally the prince hurls himself at the monster and tries to beat it with his fists and his legs. He just gets more stuck. At this point the monster tells him to give up. And the prince says, no, he will not give up, because he has a power within him which will tear them both to pieces, even if the monster devours him. At that the monster recognizes the Prince's superior courage, so he gives up and agrees to become his servant and learn from him. [1]

This peculiar tale may seem to have very little to do with the familiar attributes of nonviolent Buddhism. Yet in other respects, it has absolutely everything to do with Buddhist self-awareness and is an excellent way for us to consider the whole difficulty of letting go of ego attachments—for it takes courage to do this. We need to interpret this story as a metaphor for one of the steps that can help us to let go of the ego.

To begin with, Prince Five Weapons is in a place of successful ego: he's achieved a great deal and he feels invincible. But we are told that this is two incarnations before he becomes the Buddha, so we can be pretty sure that what he learns at this point will be a lesson that he'll need along the path to enlightenment. The monster, therefore, is not an external creature so much as the creature that comes into existence that threatens our fragile, ego-based sense of who we are. It can come at us whether we're successful princes or penniless beggars. It still seeks us out. And what it does is it shows us that our usual strengths, our five weapons, and our five senses of seeing, hearing, touching, tasting, and smelling have to face something that comes from an entirely different realm. When we are challenged by those things that exist outside our usual comfort zone, what do we do? Well, we tend to try and subdue them by using what exists within our comfort zone. Put another way, we may feel we're pretty impressive in our day-to-day world. We have some prestige, some possessions that make us look good, perhaps. Then, one day something comes along that makes all these fine attributes, our five weapons, seem useless. This is certainly what happens to Prince Five Weapons. He's a prince, he's just left his weapon master's training, he feels confident in himself as a warrior. Life is good for him. And then, in his moment of pride, he's assailed by something that doesn't obey the usual rules.

What could this mean? What is he facing? We could see this as a sort of midlife crisis, although it's actually the sort of event that can happen to any of us at any time when we're in the ego-world, because, at bottom, the monster is a representative of the fear that comes over us when we doubt our inner worth. Prince Five Weapons is a good example of this because he is, after all, a warrior. He knows he's brave, and he knows he can inflict fear on others—including terrifying them with the fear of death. In that situation, he's likely to forget his own mortality if he is thinking only of his own achievements.

Most of us aren't heroic figures, but the same lesson applies to us, too. We go along in our lives and then something happens that upends our sense of who we are. Perhaps a loved one deserts us, or we lose our job. Perhaps our children turn against us, or our boss. Sometimes this feeling manifests itself simply as the fear of death. Most people try their best to banish fear by using the five resources of the senses that have always been so good at getting us through tough times. That's one reason that depressed people go shopping, or lonely people may choose to overeat or become alcoholics. Compulsive activities of all kinds are attempts to manage uncertainty. The tactic cannot work, since the threat, the fear, comes from a psychological dimension and the proposed solution is merely a physical sop to a real need. When this happens, we are left defenseless, and we are thrown back on our own sense of personal authenticity.

Notice that Prince Five Weapons doesn't ever say exactly what it is he has that can blow both himself and the monster to smithereens. He simply asserts that what he feels in his heart is stronger than any outer threat that wishes to deprive him of it. He refuses to give up his immortal spirit and become a slave. He will not give in to fear.

This confrontation, this hand-to-hand struggle with a monster, is a component of almost every major piece of literature. Whether it's the final showdown of the gunfighters in *High Noon*, the duels at the climax of *Hamlet* and *King Lear*, St. George killing the dragon, or the final face-off between James Bond and whichever villain he faces this time around: it is essentially the same thing. In the movie of *Harry Potter and the Deathly Hallows*, Voldemort has Harry totally in his power and asks him why he lives. Harry's reply is, "Because I have something worth living for."[2] It could be straight out of the legend of Sticky Hair. How can we understand that in different terms?

The man who is being victimized by his co-workers may try everything he knows to win in the situation. He may try to placate; he may attempt to cajole. He may become angry or give way to panic; he may run and he may become vengeful. He may even "go postal" and start shooting people. But the finest thing he can do, the thing that will defeat these threats that come from the outside, is to recognize that he cannot be defeated unless he agrees to be. No one can take away his authenticity—although he may decide to give up his job and leave. This is a spiritual test that asks, in effect, are you going to live in fear or in courage? We can always choose fear, the ignoble compromise, the easy option. It's on constant special offer. But if we chose courage, then we are honoring what is authentic within ourselves; we are choosing to love ourselves.

The story, therefore, is about accessing one's courage and one's inner sense of certainty, to continue being who one is. The monster that will attack all of us is exactly like Sticky Hair. This is the monster that exists in the psyche and so can't be defeated in the conventional ways. So, the man who has lived a timid and fearful life, perhaps, may have failed to come to terms with the monster. And no amount of compensatory activity can make up for that. Of course, some people become wealthy and arrange their lives so they *seem* to be bold heroes. That's one reason some middle-aged men buy sports cars or motorcycles. But even if they do that, deep inside they know that they're not heroes, so they have to arrange another pantomime to make them temporarily feel good. Most of us in this situation will do something similar, and we'll keep doing it until we run out of "weapons"—and we'll still be left with the fear.

What this means in psychological terms is that an important part of psychic growth involves going toward one's fears and mastering them. This is not just because courage is a good thing but because going toward the thing that is the exact opposite of who one is will help us to understand the true nature of who we are. It will help to make us whole.

Each of us has fear inside us, inevitably, and this cannot be banished. But it *can* be managed. Notice that Prince Five Weapons does not parade the monster around after he's beaten it to make himself look good. He doesn't resume the ego-based pride in himself he had before. Instead, he trusts the creature to be the guardian of the scary forest he lives in. We need fear in our lives to prevent us from being arrogant and to keep us from unnecessary risks, but we also need to keep it under control.

We can always choose to ignore this sort of opportunity. People who have undergone miraculous events can choose to put them down to pure luck, or simply say they don't understand what happened. Joe Simpson survived a fall off an Andean peak and two days of crawling back to camp on a shattered thigh, alone, when everyone else in the party did not believe he could have survived. He records in his memoir *Touching The Void* that he found no significance in his terrifying adventure.[3] My own father, who met a ghost that walked through the front of his car, giving him a considerable shock, maintained until his dying day that he did not believe in ghosts. When asked to give a name to what he'd experienced he said it was a ghost, but he still said he didn't believe in them.

Similarly, we can refuse to meet our Shadow Self, which is in part what the monster Sticky Hair represents. Our Shadow Self is that part of the self that we have banished. It comes about like this. If we are competitive in our lives (and which of us isn't?), then we will learn to value those competencies that give us an edge. We may be quicker, sharper, and more decisive than our rivals, and this helps us to get what we want. But then we also have to recognize that there is, on the other side of the competitive self, a darker version of the same drive that wants to crush others, not just win; we want to annihilate the competition, not just get over the line first.

Within each of us there exists the capacity to be cruel, to smash, to destroy, even to kill. And most of the time we keep it in check, although it may emerge in our language when we watch sports events! It certainly emerges in those who engage in violent video games. This is the dark side of ourselves that most of us do not care to meet, and pretend we haven't met. Sometimes it emerges when we've had too many drinks, or when we're stressed.

Strangely enough, it also happens in traffic. We may laugh at "road rage," but encased in those insulated steel boxes called cars we can, all of us, witness every day how angry ordinary people are under certain circumstances. People shake their fists at each other and curse. Just the other day, on my town's main street, I saw two people in an altercation over whose car should have gone first. As I was watching, one man leaped from his car and hauled the other driver out, and they began a fist fight. Naturally everything stopped, and the first man's wife dragged him back.

Such uncontrolled rage! Here was a man who wasn't just over-reacting but was, in fact, helpless before his own anger. Everyone at that busy intersection saw the event, and most of us shook our heads in disbelief. For our purposes, we can notice that Prince Five Weapons finds himself totally stuck to the monster. Through this metaphor, the story shows us that the harder we fight against our recognition of the deep and lawless parts of ourselves, the more they take us over, because they actually are part of us. Given the opportunity, our primitive drives will take us over completely—unless we come to terms with them. The lesson is to learn to accept all aspects of ourselves.

In my home country, there's a well-known saying: "An Englishman's home is his castle." The situation with Sticky Hair has a flavor of that, as does the law in many parts of the United States that allows people to shoot those who break into their houses. The law acknowledges that under certain circumstances, a man may feel that he is justified in killing someone who breaks into his home. A summary death penalty as imposed by a one-person judge and jury doesn't seem quite appropriate for burglary, at least to me. Yet I too have felt this up-swelling of rage. Fortunately, when I have done, I have also been able to recognize, albeit much later at times, that I could so easily have given in to the dark force within me and gone over the line toward violence. This knowledge has helped me to grow my compassion, especially for those who have given in to rage and suffered afterward. I have been able to feel myself in their shoes.

This is what the Shadow Self is all about. It contains the parts of ourselves we don't wish to acknowledge. This is why we must get to know it, value its strength, and then keep it in its proper place. That's the courage that Prince Five Weapons shows. Since this event happens two incarnations before he becomes enlightened as the Buddha, we can see that the story contains the metaphor that tells us we must achieve the same degree of understanding as Prince Five Weapons a substantial mount of time before we can hope to reach the level of awareness that the Buddha embodies. The story shows us our path, our stepping stones over the river, for the way ahead.

Clearly, this story describes how we can meet our destructive urges and accept them. If we fail to do this, they will ambush us at various times, and they will run our lives rather than the more peaceful part of ourselves. Metaphors like this work because they offer us fictions—stories that are not to be taken literally but understood as descriptions of psychic processes.

It is worth noticing that after Sticky Hair has been defeated, he is given a trusted job as a servant and guardian. He's accepted and loved. It's a detail that recurs in several other similar myths. The suggestion is that this monster is like a rebel organization that has had to resort to extreme methods to get itself recognized, but once acknowledged, it is eager to be a part of the new government system and work peacefully in the new regime.

In recognizing this detail, we can say that at its heart the monster is loving, compassionate, and peaceful. It must be, because it can be tamed by the prince when he mobilizes his own sense of compassion. Its outer, raging aspect is simply the role it has felt itself forced to take on. And that's what anger is, really. It's a reaction to being hurt. We flare up because our sense of what is good has been injured, because we feel disregarded or undervalued. Behind even the worst offender there is, ultimately, a person who wants at some level to be loved and accepted. It may require strenuous efforts to restrain him, at least at first, but the inner need is the same.

This story, this myth, is just one example of meeting the aspects of the self we routinely try to ignore, and how we can enrich our psyche if we take the opportunity to work with them. In fact, we have many aspects of the Shadow Self we have to meet, and they come from the same series of repressed or misunderstood urges. We will take a look at some of these now. To do so we will need to know how these submerged aspects of ourselves come about.

The mechanisms of repression are fairly well known. We internalize rules and laws, as we grow up, rules that tell us to be nice and behave properly as part of our socialization. Even if we don't feel like being nice to some people, we still have to do it, and we repress our rages. In the process, we may deny that we have these feelings at all. We hide them away.

Yet there is more to consider. The tale of Sticky Hair asks us to consider how we arrive at our sense of what is "good" or acceptable. At first sight, Sticky Hair is neither; yet, as we have seen, he has much to offer. The trap that we can all fall into is that of thinking that only those things that are socially acceptable have value. This can be dangerous. There is a place for anger, of course, and there is a place for understanding, but we often don't want to look past what is on the surface. The encounter with the Shadow Self asks us to do this.

For example, we may assimilate from our cultural milieu certain understandings, perhaps that our spouse or significant other is "supposed" to be a certain way. In the United States, men are supposed to be tan, muscled, and charmingly decisive—according to Hollywood. Women are also expected to have a specific build, which includes large breasts, long legs, and usually blonde hair. Check any line of cheerleaders at a ball game, and you'll see what I mean. This is what we are aware of consciously because these facts are validated all around us every day. If we do not question these images, then we are likely to select our mate on the basis of this admittedly rather shallow set of accepted attributes and value those features highly, as long as the individual is also reasonably pleasant. This is what the culture tells us is "good." Many people run their lives this way.

But there are other forces at work, too. As we grew from tiny babies to adults, we looked at the adults around us and formed impressions from them about what a man or a woman "ought" to be. We received early psychological imprinting in this. So if our mother was a reasonably competent and loving mother we are likely to be predisposed to value women more highly if they share some of the positive traits of our mother, as we perceived them when we were small. The same thing happens with a father or father substitute, if he was loved and held in high regard.

Unfortunately, the exact same thing happens even if the parent was tyrannical and cruel. If we are not careful, we will take those early images that we have and project them onto the first person who seems to fit our personal bill, more or less, and who also corresponds to the socially accepted standards of what masculine or feminine beauty ought to be. We do this before we have any idea who the person actually is, and often people declare themselves in love very rapidly after meeting someone who seems to fit the image. They may be in love, but sometimes they are not in love with the person; instead, they are in love with what they have projected onto that person.

The images we project are those we have not examined, and don't really know. If we don't know what we're projecting, we fall every time. And why shouldn't we fall? We've set a trap for ourselves with our favorite bait already in place on the hook.

I think we've all seen this. We've all witnessed times when it's been clear that a person we know has created an image of someone that he or she is attracted to—an image that has almost nothing to do with the real person. I've done it myself, and I've been the recipient of others' projections, which has been a profoundly uncomfortable experience. This is the same sort of thing as we see when a person develops a fixation on a movie star. In such cases, the projection has run entirely out of control, and can become very unpleasant.

Psychologists call this transference. In the case of the therapist-client relationship, what gets transferred to the therapist is a series of feelings that the client has—usually unacknowledged and misunderstood feelings relating to the client's parents or early experiences. Such feelings can be extremely negative at times. For instance, the person who has problems with authority figures is very likely to be a person who couldn't work out his or her difficulties with parents, and so acts them out on any authority figure that appears. Logically it makes no sense to curse at police officers at any time, yet many men seem to do just that after too many drinks on a Saturday. They are simply projecting their rage onto a convenient figure. Today it's a police officer; tomorrow perhaps it will be a minority, a stranger, or a religious group.

One of our life-tasks, therefore, is to bring these projections to the surface and examine them so that we will not be misled by the emotions we think we feel; however, there is a more sinister level of the Shadow we have to face, for we project our submerged pain and inflict it on others unless we seek to understand the pain and stop projecting those feelings.

Some of those feelings are not actually what we want or need. No one needs to marry a clone of an abusive parent, yet this is what so often happens. Children who grew up in abusive households tend to marry abusers. Why? Because at the level of the Shadow, they recognize the familiar attributes of someone who will hurt them and they respond, even welcoming it into their lives. Every day, women are beaten and die because of this.

The Shadow is not a simple force, nor is it to be underestimated. It can be extremely dangerous. It holds within its most extreme, murkiest depths the desire to kill and also the desire to be killed. That particular force was represented in Norse myth as the beserker, the no-longer human fighter who became an out-of-control killing machine until he, too, was killed. In Shakespeare's time this figure appeared in plays as the revenger: a person so enraged by the wrongs done him that he destroyed others, even though he knew his actions would result in his own death. In our own era of "martyrs," men and women who choose to destroy themselves for their beliefs by killing others, we do not have too far to look for equivalents to such figures. This is the Shadow in its most raw and chaotic state, and even educated American citizens are not immune from such temptations. Some recent detainees are Americans who have been detected traveling to the middle east to train as martyrs, getting ready to return to the United States and wreak havoc. Under such circumstances,s we would do well to recognize the formidable power the Shadow can wield.

A less obvious form of the Shadow occurs in some cases of depression, especially when the person does not particularly care to live, and so, by extension, doesn't care who else dies, either. And so depressed and angry people shoot others and then themselves, or drive drunk and kill others. A casual scan of our news services reveals this is more common than we may want to think.

So, to sum this up so far: Unless we have gone deep into the Shadow part of ourselves to see how it works, we'll deceive ourselves in certain very dangerous ways. This doesn't answer the question, though, of how we can truly go to the place of introspection that will allow us to avoid such confusions, especially in terms of who we fall in love with. Once again, legend and myth can help us with this next step, beyond facing the monsters of our minds. Now that myth has shown us how to get fear and the destructive urges under control, it can help us deal with the exploration of the other aspects of the deep self.

CHAPTER 8

Doing the Work

Dante and the Descent
into the Dark:
Meeting the Shadow

In European mythology, this specific process of self-discovery is usually depicted as the hero literally descending into the underworld and meeting the dead. There he (for literature has far more male heroes than female ones) will meet those who have left the world and who can, therefore, see it differently and speak more openly about human experience. Whether it's in *The Odyssey* or *The Divine Comedy* or the Harry Potter tales (in which Harry frequently visits past events), the first part of this process involves going into a netherworld that allows the traveler (and the reader) to think differently about the nature of the everyday world.

This is a very ancient pattern. One of the earliest recorded myths we have, from ancient Sumer, tells of the supreme goddess Inanna descending from her realm to the underworld, the land of death, which is ruled by her enemy. This is no ordinary enemy, though, since it is her sister Ereshkigal, whom she fears will kill her. On the way to find her, Inanna passes through seven gates, and is at each one forced to shed some of the regal finery of which she is so proud, until she is naked. It's an interesting echo of Prince Five Weapons finding his fighting skills to be useless against Sticky Hair. Just similarly, Inanna's descent seems to involve the stripping away of the ego. [1] This myth is important for us because Sumerian myths are the basis of so many later middle eastern religious stories, including the Bible, and so it can be seen as one of the earliest references we have to what has since become a very familiar pattern.

We'll be looking at a more recent story here, specifically Dante's *Divine Comedy*. I've chosen it because it is to some extent representative of all the stories of descending into the depths of the self and why this might be spiritually necessary. Written between A.D.1308 and 1321, it has moved countless generations of readers—a sure sign it may have something useful to tell us.

Of course, Dante's story is extremely dramatic: a descent into Hell, then the ascent to Heaven. I'm not suggesting we all have to go through something as drastic, although those who have undergone disasters have often come through, renewed, on the other side feeling that they have been through hell. Many consider themselves blessed to have had such difficulties. What I'd like you to notice is that Dante's story tells us in detail what we can expect to find when we look inside ourselves. Some of what we find may not be very pleasant, and we'll come up against all those selfish ego tendencies we all have.

Dante's message is clear, though: he asks us to observe what the tendencies are that keep these poor souls stuck in Hell. When we see these failings in others, we can know them, avoid them, and as we learn from them we will grow in compassion. For we will see that these faults lie within each of us, too. Only then can we move beyond these ego-longings that will stop us from experiencing synchronicity.

Dante gives us a mythic structure—one we are invited to consider deeply and from which we can learn. In the poem, Dante is led through Hell by the poet Virgil and witnesses an array of suffering sinners who are truly ghastly. Again and again, Dante meets sinners who have chosen the selfish way forward, and in Hell, their punishment is that they have to repeat that choice forever. The financial thieves, for example, spend eternity pushing around huge boulders, totally intent on what they're doing. Since that was a version of what they chose in life, as they selfishly ignored real people in favor of their work, they now get to choose it again in death.

Be careful what you choose, Dante seems to say, because you may get stuck with it forever. This is a surprisingly modern way to think of evil and punishment. As we travel through the circles of Hell with Dante we see that, over and over again, the inmates chose their sin in the world of the living, and now they suffer because they are forced to stay with that sin in Hell, choosing it eternally. I'm reminded of the Wall Street bandits of recent times who continued to go after more and more money, even when it was clear they had nothing much of significance to spend it on. Sin, for Dante, seems to be about choosing selfishly rather than deciding to turn back to God. It's about opting for ego gratification and ignoring others.

We can translate this example to our modern world. Haven't we all chosen selfishly and told little lies because of it? Most people, according to surveys regularly reported in the press, will cheat just a little on their taxes and will try to benefit financially on their expense accounts, if they have them.

Most people would normally be ashamed of these little evasions and dishonesties, but we all think we won't be found out. That's what makes us lie to ourselves. We all have the tendency to do it. The tendency doesn't matter; the question is whether we'll give in. The same thing is true when it comes to choosing to be in the flow of life. We may respect it, in theory, but we are all tempted to choose the other route. When we put our ego first we disrupt the energy of synchronicity. Dante equates this flow with God's love, and sees those suffering souls as having turned away from its embrace. His vocabulary is different, but the message is essentially the same.

Reading Dante, I'm reminded of the time I spent working in a maximum security jail teaching literature to "lifers," many of whom were murderers. At first I thought that I'd just use the literature to appeal to the best part of these men, since I could never commit a violent crime, surely? But very soon after I started to teach there I recognized that, but for the grace of God, I too could easily have found myself in a situation where I might have done something desperate. I was not separate from them; I was all too like them. I just hadn't been tested or tempted to their limit, to their breaking point. These men truly understood Macbeth's descent into murder and madness, for example, and his drive not to turn back under any circumstances.

This is exactly the flavor that comes through Dante's description of Hell. We see these sinners suffering, and we can, without too much trouble, recognize that we too might have wound up that way. For us, the readers, it is important that we recognize the temptations so that we can arrange to avoid them in future. Dante is teaching us a valuable lesson about ourselves, if we wish to hear it. As we descend into ourselves we have to accept these lawless parts of our psyche as attributes that arise inevitably from the ego-self. We have to recognize them as ours and still keep them under control. We have to reach out and touch Hell and burn our fingers. Only then can we understand in our hearts, fully, how the ego leads us astray. This is something we cannot do if we simply consider things intellectually, which is why Dante gave us a poem that moves our emotions. Giving in to these ego-temptations can only move us away from the centeredness that allows us to be in tune with synchronicity.

A good example of how this works is in Canto V, for instance, when Dante meets the lovers Paolo and Francesca, and weeps at their fate. The poet, though, is masterful in his description, since as we read we notice that Francesca only speaks of her own sorrow and how she feels she and Paolo have been wronged. Not for a moment does she acknowledge that she betrayed her husband and Paolo betrayed his own brother when they gave in to their passion, which then led to their deaths. Reading her words, we can empathize with their dreadful situation, and also be aware that they see themselves as blameless. They feel they are helpless victims rather than rational people who had choices. It's not what the lovers did that shocks Dante; it's their blindness to the moral consequences of their actions. Ego-justifications like theirs, the blaming of others for what is essentially their own situation, is something we all know—and these are truly seductive excuses Dante shows us.

Dante returns to this theme several times, on each occasion with increasing emphasis, and specifically in Canto XXXIII. There we see Count Ugolino doing the same thing as Francesca, blaming another for his fate, except in this instance as he does so he's also attacking the back of Archbishop Ruggieri's head, mauling it using only his teeth. When he pauses from this ghastly action in order to speak, he focuses on how cruelly he was punished by Ruggieri; and indeed his fate was a cruel one. He and four of his sons and grandsons were jailed and then left to starve to death. What Ugolino fails to mention is that he had already betrayed another grandson, and with him his political party and his own city, which led directly to his own weakened political situation and imprisonment; so Ugolino is actually responsible for the situation that kills them all. In his self-justifications he cannot, and will not, see his own responsibility. His ego is outraged at the way he feels he has been treated; and so he remains, still trapped in his ego, deep in hell, blaming others.

Later in this book, I will take the time to examine some more of the ways we can fall into unproductive ego-spaces, places in which we can lose our way, just like Dante's poor sufferers. Our advantage is that we have the chance to get out of those spaces. Forewarned is forearmed.

If we stay with Dante for a moment, we discover he has far more to say about this descent into the self. In the poem, Dante and Virgil leave Hell by going to its uttermost depths and scrambling out on the other side of the earth, where everything is now the other way up. It's a wonderful metaphor. Hell, he seems to say, is the precise reverse of how we could choose to see things. If we just shift our gaze, we won't have to be drawn into sins and other things that will torture our minds with misery. The things we are so attached to, the comforters of the ego, are simply not important when seen from a different angle. Hell is not just a place; as we've seen, it's also a frame of mind.

As Dante proceeds, he leaves the realm of men and sin far behind, as if it were another dimension, and under the care of Beatrice he finds his way toward Heaven and the Virgin Mary. Whether we believe in a Christian worldview or not, the psychic process Dante describes is important. Dante, we notice, is now in a more female world. He's not only the opposite way up but also in the realm of the opposite sex. Virgil, the male poet, has guided Dante, the male poet, through Hell and through Purgatory, but Virgil cannot take Dante all the way on this spiritual journey: the pure saintly Beatrice, a woman, is the only one who can guide Dante forward now.

To spell this out simply: the idealized virginal Beatrice leads the poet to the ideal female, the pure mother symbol of the Virgin Mary. What Dante learns after understanding the destructive part of himself and rejecting it, leaving it behind in Hell, is that only then can his real salvation be found, in this opposite-sex world of gentleness and love. He's moved from a realm of punishment to a realm of compassion, and eventually one of unconditional love. He has met the opposite of himself, the female anima, if we use Jungian terms, and has allowed it to transform him. The language is religious, the metaphor universal.

For Dante, the process of becoming fully spiritually aware involves understanding sin and its attractions, noticing that good works are not enough (in Purgatory), and then, finally, accepting that he has the capacity to love unconditionally. He loves and is loved, and so he moves into a new relationship with God. His poem is the expression of that relationship.

So far, then, between these two very different tales of Dante and Prince Five Weapons, which I have chosen because they are representative of many others like them, we can see that descending into the self means, first of all, finding the limitations of the ego-world and not giving in to fear when we see the ego-world won't supply all our needs. It means stepping outside ourselves.

Second, it also involves taking a moral inventory of ourselves and seeing how our ego claims can lead us toward inauthentic and selfish living—which Dante shows us as sin. We must acknowledge the lawless parts of ourselves and accept that there is real energy in these urges. If we accept these urges we can use this energy without giving in to their destructive aspects. This means that, instead of responding with selfishness, we mobilize compassion that we perhaps didn't know we had, and we respect all human beings just a little bit more as a result. Compassion always means that we love others because we see that we are exactly as they are—even if they have gone farther along that destructive path than we have. We are not different.

Third, the tales seem to show us that we have to let go of wanting to be right so we can embrace the softer aspects of ourselves that we so often ignore or discard. This quality is love in its highest form, which lets us live confidently in the flow of creation, or the presence of God. In Jungian terms, Dante has to meet and be redeemed by his anima, the female aspects of himself embodied in the saintly Beatrice, that as a male he has had to repress. Until he has met the anima, he is not a complete soul, not fully balanced.

For women, the trajectory is exactly the same, except that the task is to meet the animus, the loving male energy within. The animus and anima can best be understood as figures that personify or embody certain positive attributes we need to welcome back into our lives. They show us what we have to do. Seeing them as actual people is simply a convenient way to visualize a psychic process.

The Grimm fairy tale "The Skillful Huntsman" offers a good example of this. In the tale, the huntsman manages to break into a castle in the dead of night where he plans to abduct the sleeping princess. Outside the castle gates are three enormous, totally immoral giants, who are waiting for him to commit his lawless deed. It's a scene that echoes the descent into the dark regions of the Shadow, with its lawless passions. But the huntsman sees the innocence and beauty of the princess, and he decides instead to kill the giants using a magic sword he finds in the castle. Then he leaves without telling anyone what he's done, taking only the sword, and a slipper, a scarf, and a corner cut from the princess's nightshirt.

The princess, in her vulnerable state, could be an immense temptation to this man so well versed in killing. Fortunately for him, he is moved when he sees her, and his conversion to morality is what happens when the softer emotions evoked by this anima figure are acknowledged as a vital part of his life. He decides to control his lawless urges and use the power he finds there, symbolized by the sword, to defeat what is evil rather than to pursue ego gratification. This man, a killer of animals, is tempted to worse crimes but, instead, uses his ability to kill only in order to do what is right. This elegant and succinct tale reflects precisely the psychic process we are looking at here. The specific mementos from the castle that the Huntsman chooses now serve as reminders of the moral life he must lead from now on.

During my time working within the prisons of Massachusetts, I saw examples of similar actions. Hardened older cons would sometimes take time to teach younger inmates how to survive, showing them what to avoid, helping them to take education programs or rehab courses, watching over them so they could do their time without getting into worse trouble. It didn't always work, but when it did the process was transformative for the older and the younger convicts.

For most of us, the animus and anima are hard to comprehend until we consider that in real life, we often meet people who have admirable qualities. When we do, we may decide to become a bit more like them in certain ways. We may meet many such people and be inspired by them, and in each instance we grow our animus or anima aspects as a result. Similarly, we may meet people who are fragile and innocent, and this can bring out our caring qualities as we respond to their trusting and unsuspecting natures. The result is that we become more loving and trusting. In dreams, however, the process can become radically simplified, concentrated into a meeting with just one figure—literature tends to do the same thing.

This is all very well as a generalized moral map, of course, but we don't all have the opportunity to be guided through Hell, Purgatory, and Paradise. So how are we to make this epic descent into ourselves to uncover who we truly are? How do we learn unconditional love? How does Dante's mythic tale apply in our lives?

One woman put it this way, when she found herself in the synchronicity of a blossoming career at the age of 60. She said that she knew she now had good things to convey to the world that she simply didn't have access to in her twenties and thirties. She said that she'd "put in her thirty years in the trenches," and that this experience of the dark, the difficult, and the uncertain was what now gave her the drive to do the work she felt called to do. She'd faced just about everything she felt the world could throw at her and survived, and now she knew her strength.

That's a pretty good description of the descent into the self and the re-emergence back into life. It doesn't always have to be quite as hard as her descent seems to have been. "In the trenches" suggests the horrors of World War One, after all. But we can learn from her, and from Dante.

Now, at this point you may be thinking this all sounds rather frightening—that I'm going to make you go deep into some scary place that will feel like a trial by fire. So let me reassure you—we won't be doing that. There's a straightforward reason for this: we don't have to go there because in all probability you've already visited that place. Some of you know this. Perhaps you've been through life-threatening events, diseases, tragedies, disasters, miracles. You know you've been through some strange experiences. Yet there are others of you who may not know it, because the events may seem to have been "ordinary." I'm going to show you that there is nothing "ordinary" about those less dramatic events. They all have the capability of breaking us open to see what we need to see.

Some people are only ever broken open to become more loving by undergoing experiences that are literally "shattering." Others are opened in a gentler way, as a flower opens in sunlight.

Opening up is, fortunately, often much less complicated than Dante's poem suggests—as long as we're aware of what is going on. That is the key. That means seeing our human experience as a reflection of something eternal.

So, let me give you an everyday example of the way we descend into ourselves. When we fall deeply in love we may discover depths of longing, need, and tenderness we never knew we had, and we may discover depths of courage we never knew we could access when we have to struggle to gain the partner of our affections. Men may find they possess real tenderness, for the first time; and women may find themselves able to be more powerful than they had thought they were allowed to be. These may be stereotypical examples of what happens, but it describes what can happen when each sex contacts the animus or anima.

It is no accident that Dante, the poet of worldly Florence, chose Beatrice as his guide to Heaven, a woman he loved from afar in nonsexual and idealized ways. Earthly love is just a shadowy reflection of the love of God, as Dante conveys it, just as when we fall in love with someone we may, if we're alert, begin to see the holiness that is always present in such imperfect unions. Honoring that holiness is what changes experience into real wisdom.

In fact, making contact with one's Shadow Self, and then with the anima or animus, is an essential component of falling in love. Choosing a life partner involves real choice, a genuine decision to yield the freedom of being unattached to the desire for connection. It involves accepting and surrendering certain aspects of one's ego self and moving toward other, more loving aspects of ourselves. The psychological shift generally follows this pattern. We learn that it is not all about us, that we are part of something bigger. The switch of emphasis from "I" to "the relationship" is huge, and many struggles occur when one partner puts the "I" before the "we."

Even if our love life is less than perfect, there are even more powerful examples of this process available to us. Most people learn important life lessons when they fall in love with their infant children, or learn to care for others who need their help. The large macho man may find himself moved by unexpected tenderness at the innocent fragility of his child or at the frailty of an aging parent. In that moment, he is making contact with some of the elements he may have had to repress during his normal daytime life—the tenderness he cannot display at the workplace, perhaps, or the warm love that his normally jovial colleagues might regard as sentimental. He is contacting the innocent, loving nature in himself at this time, the anima.

Similarly a woman may discover, in caring for her children, the reserves of energy and determination that may have been pushed aside in her responses to what social norms "expect" a woman to be. She can contact her determined and practical self, the animus or male component of herself that she too has been required to suppress. This, or an event like it, can be the spur that causes men and women to acknowledge the positive values of the opposite qualities to those they are usually asked to exhibit, and by contacting those qualities they can grow as people. It is as if people who had been forced to live their lives with one hand tied were suddenly allowed to admit that the other hand exists and can be used.

But what we are considering goes even deeper. It occurs when the exhausted parent realizes that, yes, she probably would give her life for her child if push came to shove. It is when the man realizes he would fight to the death to save his family. He does not have to do this, he just has to know he would willingly choose it.

If we want another example of this, then just think of all the single mothers in the world who take on the heroic task of raising their children alone, being both father and mother, and doing the job successfully, too. At such times, these women have the opportunity to reach the balance of male and female, animus and anima, and it is neither an easy task nor a one-time action. It has to be retained and lived through the years. In archetypal terms, we are looking at the balance of the Warrior-Lover archetype.

Of course, it's never enough just to fall in love with one's infant child. That's relatively easy. What is at issue here is the act of loving the child throughout a lifetime, through difficulties and fights and misunderstandings. The experience of parenting will bring the adult back into contact with all the difficulties of his or her own childhood, and all the buried fears and wants and sadness that have been repressed. Facing these issues, while trying to be the best parent one can be—that's a descent to meet the Shadow Self. What we discover as we parent is just how difficult the task can be. At those moments, we are offered the opportunity to understand our own parents and their struggles, perhaps for the first time. When we see them like this, as human, frail, fallible, that's when resentments turn to compassion and love. They were doing the best they knew how at the time, being loving in their own strange ways. We see the loving heart at the center of the monster Sticky Hair.

Jung's concept of the animus and anima is based on the images his clients spontaneously produced, which we will see are plentifully echoed in myth and literature. Just as the frightening outside of Sticky Hair concealed the loving inside, so too the stereotypical "male" and "female" attributes of the animus and anima reveal the loving core of each human being: these two concepts are essentially the same recognition. For what each person has to do is access his or her courage and his or her sense of compassion, both of them powered by love, and these are actions that will be different for every person.

Animus and anima are psychological terms that fit the "typical" person, and they suffer in clarity as a result. Perhaps a better way to describe them is to see them as aspects of what we might call the "non-ego." When we give up ego, we contact that part of ourselves that connects us to everyone else. The mere fact of falling in love or of having children, or caring for others is not enough; the point is to be able to see the deep significance of the event, be changed by it, and to remember that these lessons are basically lessons in how to be a more loving human being—lessons that need to be remembered everyday and in every circumstance.

These lessons may sound ordinary, but the whole point here is to see that they are not. They have mythic significance as points at which the soul can grow. We can understand this by looking at the opposite of this way of living. Just think of the cliché of the commitment-avoidant man, who flees from settled relationships or the possibility of family. We'd have to say that a person like this is thoroughly frightened; that's why he (or sometimes she) runs away. Committing to a relationship means being vulnerable and overcoming fear not just once but as a component of daily living. This means taking on responsibilities, being open with one's partner, challenging him or her, being honest about oneself, and dealing with the demands of the outside world, too. That takes real courage. It takes us to our limits, to our breaking points. During the course of any committed relationship, we will encounter serious situations and reach our limits; we will feel despair and be tempted to give up and run. That is a descent into Hell. And we can grow from the experience.

The daughter of a friend comes to mind here. She has an autistic child and has been tested by having to cope with this condition and what it demands from her, as well as what she has had to give up in terms of her career hopes. Facing this challenge has not been easy; yet, anyone who meets her knows, right away, that here is a person who has moved through the deep waters of fear and doubt and even of anger and disappointment. She has put aside her ego-based hopes and has come to a profoundly loving place. She's had her descent into the depths and emerged empowered. She knows her strengths, and she knows what it means to come close to giving up. But she hasn't.

Perhaps Winston Churchill put it best, in his wonderfully laconic statement, "If you're going through Hell, keep going."

One of the things we'll be doing in the pages ahead is taking the time to assess the traps we can fall into—which Dante illustrates for us as the Sinners in Hell—so that we don't have to make mistakes that come from the ego. This also means recognizing that those failings are not "out there," but within us. We'll realize that Dante's observations apply to us, too. We'll have to make that descent into ourselves, putting aside the ego, taking a moral inventory of ourselves, and then contact the opposite part, the non-ego of ourselves, so that we can activate the full abilities of the completed self. This is the way to find ourselves in the flow, in the space of synchronicity.

The Mythological Aspect

As evidence to support what I've been saying about the redeeming power of children, we can refer to the great myths and legends of our civilization. The arrival of children has been seen for countless generations as the start of a process that involves opening up the heart. Perhaps the most startling version is the idea of the Virgin Birth. This is not just a Christian idea; it existed in Greek mythology, too. Athena, the cerebral goddess, springs fully formed from the side of Zeus' head, in a particularly powerful version of Virgin Birth. Even before the Greeks took up this idea, it had appeared in Egyptian mythology, with Iris conceiving from the dead mummified body of Osiris, in an interesting variant of the miraculous birth motif. American Indian creation stories also have many variants of the Virgin Birth. [2]

If we take Virgin Birth as fact, we are in a space of very curious biology; but if we see it as a metaphor it can tell us something about who were are. The Virgin Birth, where the God energy impregnates a pure woman, can be seen as a metaphor for the internal rebirth that awaits each of us when we align with divine energy and allow our more loving side to be fueled by it. When we let the divine into our lives we are spiritually reborn from within.

This is a metaphor, but it supports the experience of what happens when a man is turned into a profoundly loving force on the birth of his child: the mother and child are seen as something more miraculous than he could have believed possible beforehand. You don't have to go far to see this. Just wait until someone you know has a child and observe what seems to be happening psychically within those parents. Watch, and you'll see that these people who are new parents will be stunned by what they've become part of. Now you could put that down to the drama of the event, the sense of responsibility that comes with it, or any number of other factors. But I'm willing to bet that the myth is being lived out right in front of you. Hearts are being opened.

The Virgin Birth is a metaphor for the purity that is born within each of us when we learn to feel love and put ego aside. The Persian poet Rumi uses the idea eloquently. Perhaps surprisingly for a Sufi of the 13th century, in his poem "Soul, Heart and Body one Morning," Rumi uses a specifically Christian reference ("Mary, miraculously pregnant") to describe that moment of marvelous change that can wash over each of us. But his listeners would have understood exactly what he meant:

> There's a morning where presence comes over you
> And you sing like a rooster in your earth-colored shape.
> Your heart hears and, no longer frantic, begins
> To dance. At that moment soul Reaches total emptiness.
> Your heart becomes Mary,
> Miraculously pregnant, and body, like a two-day-old
> Jesus says wisdom words. [3]

"The presence comes over you," the poet says. He's describing what happens when we move into alignment with the power of God or the Universe and miracles happen in our awareness, in our lives. Synchronicity opens itself to us—we speak miraculous words like a two-day-old Jesus, as we find ourselves flooded by transcendence.

When transcendent moments happen we may be frightened by their strangeness. We may try to run. We may deny that they occur. Yet the poet tells us that there's nothing to fear—the heart is "no longer frantic"—and we allow what is holy to be acknowledged. That's good advice for anyone, especially the man holding his child.

And here's the point. Myth doesn't predict what anyone will feel. When it appears in this way, in poetry, it offers a framework that supports people in their feelings and gives them, in effect, validation for the processes they are going through—which might otherwise be bewildering. Myth helps us to pay attention to what we feel, so that we'll know we're feeling it and be able to value it. It gives us a framework for our experiences to become meaningful.

CHAPTER 9

Myth and Literature

The Ancient Forms of the Descent
and their Value for Us

The concept of the descent into the underworld is probably as old as mythology itself and exists in almost all cultures in one form or another. We've already considered the myth of the goddess Inanna, but there is another version of this tale, more widely disseminated, that is almost as ancient. This is the story of Hades and Persephone.

Hades, the god of the underworld, sees Persephone walking one day and abducts this beautiful maiden to his underworld kingdom. Her mother Demeter, who is the goddess of the harvest, is so upset she refuses to make the crops grow and the earth fruitful until, eventually, she manages to reclaim her daughter. Even so, Persephone is allowed to spend only part of the year above ground, because she has been tricked into eating a pomegranate and some seeds have remained in her teeth. Some legends say four, some say six seeds remain, and these match the number of months she must return to the underworld each year, and therefore to the length of time that the earth must remain barren. This corresponds directly to the different climates and the length of time during which the soil is productive. The seeds in her teeth, obviously, are things that rightly belong in the soil, below ground, so the symbolism is appropriate.

If this myth were simply a story to explain why the earth has seasons, it would be useful. Yet it also includes certain important extra attributes, to do with understanding that the earth has fruitful seasons and fallow seasons, and that when the fields are barren there is still something important happening in the soil, since the death of one season leads to new life later. It is therefore a depiction of the cycle of life and death and renewal that affects the food source, and it also tells us that we are part of this cycle. It says, in effect, that there is a Divine Rhythm that we have to become attuned

65

to if we wish to be part of the cosmic plan. It therefore points toward a basic form of synchronicity.

This is only the surface, however, because the myth says, in effect, that since this is the cycle of renewal, if we are to renew ourselves spiritually we too will need to return to the depths, the source, and encounter what is there, so we can be reborn.

If we add to this the significant fact that Persephone is female, and that the Oracle at Delphi was controlled by priestesses, we have a sense of the descent involving a meeting with a powerful female figure who is in touch with the way ahead, a prophetess. In Greek life, women were not held in high esteem except for their roles as priestesses, and the priestess at Delphi (called the Pythia) was one of the very highest of appointments. There, the woman who was the receiver of the Oracle sat at the inmost sanctum of the temple, over a fissure in the ground from which subterranean vapors arose, and, intoxicated by these vapors, she would prophesy. She was consulted respectfully by male rulers who needed divine guidance. Before the men could get to this sanctum, though, they had first to thread their way past various memorials that praised the power of gods in giving human beings success or victory. It was a trip designed to humble the ego.

The temple of the oracle at Delphi therefore presents us with a physical image of the penetration to the mysterious realm of the underworld, where the seeker encounters a strange female figure, and the subsequent return to the ordinary world with the message she has relayed to the male seeker. We could hardly ask for a clearer metaphor.

This entire process is echoed in the highly secret ancient Eleusinian Mysteries, of which we know very little. If this sounds abstruse, bear in mind that the Eleusinian Mysteries were a powerful religion in the Mediterranean for 2,000 years before Christianity came along and displaced it. These were myths that worked, and that people felt to be vital, for a very long time. [1]

What we do know is that there were two levels of participation in the ceremonies, and at the highest level the initiate would enter a dark place and meet priests dressed as various figures. These included Persephone and Pluto, making them the obvious representations of the underworld, and then Hercules dressed in female clothing. This seems to reinforce the theme we've been considering that links the male/female balance with the balancing of animus/anima. This is important because initiates would have been both men and women, so an anima figure alone would not have been enough.

The next figures encountered in this ceremony were Castor and Pollux, the mythological twins, one of whom was immortal and the other was not. So far, then, the initiates have been faced first with representations that would cause them to reconsider the polarization of sexual opposites of male and female, and then with the divine opposites of mortal and immortal. It seems clear they were asked to see themselves as part of this continuum rather than as just one or the other of a pair of opposites. We are, each of us, a mix of male and female attributes, and a blend of immortal consciousness and all-too mortal physical form. As they emerged from this the initiates then met the figure of Apollo, whose music was an echo of the music of the spheres. Of course, music has to do with time and rhythm, and in this circumstance suggests the divine rhythms of synchronicity. Thus, the ceremony reenacted a profound psychic truth of personal rebirth in exactly the way we have been discussing, leading to a unity with the divine.

In each case we've looked at there is a descent of some sort, a meeting with the anima or animus, and a return. This is the basic pattern.

If we recall for a moment the stories of King Alfred, Tamerlane, and Robert the Bruce that I mentioned at the beginning of this book, what we see is the outline of the same myth. In each story, a king is brought low by despair and comes into contact with Nature in its humblest form—an ant, a spider, a poor woman making oatcakes. From these encounters, each man draws inspiration and renewal, and each takes action that brings about the desired result. Each tale deals with the descent into the self. Each is a metaphor of the need to contact the anima, and through that encounter to experience the divine rhythm, for it is only this which can lead them to success. Each is a story of finding synchronicity.

Once we begin to notice this myth, it appears in many places. That is a good indication that this is one of the deep structures of the psyche, revealed to us through story and myth, for thousands of years. [2] The ancient Greeks even differentiated between the concepts of the descent into the depths and simply visiting the dead. The reason for this is that each event tells us we can learn profound truths about ourselves in two different ways. We can learn the hard way, through full immersion, or the easy way. The choice is ours. But we can't move into synchronicity without the lesson.

This may all seem rather theoretical, so I'll give you some concrete evidence to back up this claim for the descent into the self. Literature has helped us to explain ourselves to ourselves for millennia. That's why it has survived. And literature refers frequently to the descent into the self, but we don't always see it.

I thought I knew all about this aspect of literature—until I had my own descent into the darkness of the self. At the time I was working with disturbed adolescents in England, in a wonderful experimental residence that now no longer exists. It was extraordinary work, very taxing, and I was not prepared for it. What happened was that I became ill. My mind wouldn't admit that I'd got into something that was too much for me, so my body had to tell me. I developed a lung condition and became so ill that I nearly died. My ego wanted me to be a success and was prepared to kill me to prevent me from seeing that this type of work, under these circumstances, was too much for me. When I began to see what I was doing to myself, I knew that, quite simply, I'd come up against my limits and I'd better respect them. The ego had to back down. I was like a mid-distance runner taking part in a marathon. I just wasn't a good fit for this work.

It took me months of illness and suffering and doubt and fear to reach this simple conclusion. Years later I discovered that the lungs, in Chinese medicine, are the seat of grief. This was completely congruent with my spiritual journey. My refusal to admit that I'd made a mistake, my dogged insistence that I would be a success at this type of career, my pride, all these had a great deal to do with the deeper grief I felt at what I perceived as my father's failure to see who I actually was. My wounded ego was in mourning for a relationship that wasn't happening.

My return to health occurred because I went, in despair, to visit an acupuncturist. The clinic took me in, and within a week I was much improved. Conventional medicine had failed me, but energy medicine had no trouble turning me around. I was astonished, since acupuncture was not respectable in 1980s England. This meant I had to rethink my relationship medicine and to my body, too. Toward the end of my treatment, the dear lady who was working with me, Mrs. Williamson, said, "Oh, we only ever had one person who was more ill than you come to us. He lived, too."

It had been a close call.

At the time I didn't know what was going on. Now I can see that I had gone through the descent. I'd met my anger, my sadness, my limitations, and realized that I wanted to live anyway. Conventional medicine had not worked so, like Dante finding Hell turned upside down as he left it to enter Purgatory, I had to move into another dimension of thinking and being. In the process, I cracked my armored soul wide open.

There are no hard lessons; there are only hard ways to learn them.

Years later, I realized that this sort of soul experience is at the heart of almost all great literature, and of quite a lot of bad literature, too. The main character gets tested and has to learn a few things, a few vital human lessons, about loving himself and others. If I'd known that at the time, I think I could have saved myself a lot of sadness, despair, shame, and time. The experience had been there, described in many instances on the pages, but I'd missed it entirely. Now I can see that the great books I thought I knew so well had a message for me that I had missed altogether in my pride. I needed to get acquainted with my negative energies, so that they didn't run my life, and I needed to find my anima, so that I could love others more fully. Painful as it was, this turned out to be one of the most beneficial lessons of my life.

There's no single way of living this experience, no "official" way forward. Myth and literature often say similar things in different ways. Sometimes it's done so gently that we hardly even notice what's going on until we stop to think about it. So let's look at a few examples of how men and women meet the animus and anima.

Since we've looked at Dante, we may as well continue with one of the greatest writers of all time: Shakespeare. In his great comedies of role changing, the female lead dresses as a boy in order to instruct the man she loves on how to love her, which always means in a more sensitive way. This is the main theme of *As You Like It*, *Twelfth Night*, and *The Merchant of Venice*. It's present in a different way in *All's Well That Ends Well*, too, where Helena succeeds in civilizing everyone, except her husband. The women become men in order to access their own strength and to educate the men to be more sensitive to women. Animus and anima are activated in the process. It can't happen, though, until the men find themselves thwarted, desperate, and unable to proceed with their specific ego-plans. They have to languish in their own version of hell for a while. Only then do they start listening.

Even though this theme is used as a convenient device of romantic comedy, the overall effect is that the man has to learn to moderate his pursuit of the woman to whom he is attracted. He often only sees her as an idealized abstract, and in that mind-frame he lays manly siege to her heart in a way that is a cliché of the customs of the time. Instead, he has to learn how to participate in a dialogue with her—to listen to her, learn from her, and let go of his male posturing. He can't do this, however, until he has reached a moment of despair. Only when he moves away from his old ego-self can he earn her, and only when that happens can she throw off her protective disguise—the thing that stops her from being a real woman.

Now, we can choose to see this as Shakespeare making a point about the social constructs of what is male and what is female amid the stereotyping of his time. And this would be true. But we can also notice him pointing out that this is a vital step that men and women must undertake in order for them to lay a strong foundation of self-awareness on which to build their lives together. In fact, he seems to be saying that unless men can access their female side, and women can access their male side, the future is unlikely to be happy; furthermore, they are only able to do this when they are forced to let go of their familiar roles, when life lets them down and drops them into despair. Shakespeare, we may wish to notice, was writing 300 years before Jung formulated his psychological explanations.

If we need further illustrations of this, we have only to look at Shakespeare's trag-edies. These have many traits, but one of the most straightforwardly noticeable is that when men and women either don't listen to each other or become polarized, disaster ensues. King Lear doesn't listen to any of his daughters, then he banishes the one who speaks pure and true love, thereby destroying them both. Hamlet rejects the weak-willed Ophelia and his even less impressive mother—and all three wind up dead. Brutus won't listen to anyone, let alone his wife, so he ends up as defeated as Caesar, who also wouldn't listen to anyone, and certainly not to his wife's prophetic advice. In contrast, Macbeth does listen to his wife, but she is busy trying to persuade him that he can't be a real man unless he kills his king. It's a travesty of the actual understandings of what a man ought to be. Lady Macbeth has had to force herself to believe this ghastly parody of manhood, then uses sexual blackmail to make her husband do her will. The two sexes are out of balance, and instead of humanizing and moderating each other they drive each other into murderous psychosis.

The list could go on if we scan all Shakespeare's tragedies, since it's present in all of them. What we need to notice here is that Shakespeare saw just how important this descent into the self was, and how we all have to meet the repressed values of the opposite sex in ourselves so we can learn from them and incorporate them. We then have to remain in touch with what we've learned and carry it through our lives (just as we'd remain close to a spouse). The vital point is that we only get to meet our op-posite when we have descended to the place of helplessness and spiritual bleakness, when we have to start listening because we've tried everything else.

This is mirrored by the actual psychological processes we can see around us. Many people I have worked with in counseling have begun to reconstruct their shattered lives only because everything they have held dear thus far, every agreement and sense of purpose they ever lived by, has failed them. Sometimes a catastrophe can have good results. I know. I've been through it.

Shakespeare makes this point in the comedies we've been considering as well as in his last complete play, *The Tempest*. There the aging, exiled, Prospero has been forced to see his failings, and in his isolation he has been humanized by his innocent daughter Miranda (an anima figure, certainly). Finally, when those who exiled him appear on his island, he has to fight against his desire for revenge. Compassion wins out and, at the end, he gives up control of the island by renouncing his magic. When he does so—and not until then—the synchronous events happen that bring the story to completion and harmony. When we let go of our ego-desires, when we stop trying to control things and open our hearts to love and compassion, then the synchronous forces take over.

It's a pattern Shakespeare repeated successfully in *Twelfth Night*, *As You Like It*, and *All's Well*. The plot reaches, in each case, a point at which the human beings involved in it cannot solve the problems—and so the problems miraculously solve themselves. Interestingly enough, not all of the characters agree to these resolutions. Malvolio, Bertram, and Jaques all reject the happy endings. Some people will always be blind to synchronicity.

The trouble is that when we use Shakespeare's plays as a point of comparison—especially those comedies—we find they depend upon some very particular circumstances to get the characters to learn about life. What happens if we don't find someone to instruct us? What happens if the person we find ourselves attracted to and perhaps married to has never made this tricky descent into the self, and so is just as ignorant about the need to do so as we are?

The answer seems to be that there are no free rides. Those who don't find a worthy partner with whom they can navigate these difficult waters still get to go on the journey. For there are always two levels to all love relationships. The first is of the body, and the second is of the spirit; it is the second of these that we are talking about. If there is no spiritual component available for the marriage, the couple will drift apart, and in the resulting sadness they may each find the opportunity to tackle the descent into themselves. Some people will fight against it, perhaps using alcohol, drugs, or compulsive behaviors to try and keep the emptiness at bay. But the emptiness is always there, waiting for us to deal with it.

This is why we need art. The wisdom in art, story, myth, and literature is available for anyone, no matter how inexperienced that person may be in other ways. But that also means we have to pay attention and be prepared to learn from art—not just regard it as an evening's forgettable entertainment.

Let's look at a few more examples to see what clues these sources may have for us about our mental processes. In Greek myth, Orpheus descends to the underworld to reclaim his dead wife Eurydice, in a legend that has been told and repeated many times. Just before they reach the surface and its welcome normality, Orpheus makes a fatal error: he looks back over his shoulder. Having been expressly forbidden to do so, as a condition of being allowed to reclaim his wife, Eurydice is whisked back down to the underworld again.

As a metaphor, what this conveys to us is that we can contact our opposite self, animus or anima, but that we can equally easily lose contact with what we know in our hearts when we come back to the everyday world. We "forget," or we deny, or we discount what we know to be true in the depths of our being. It's easy to do. We turn away from what actually is right for us and accept instead what everyone else thinks is right for us.

In Book 11 of Homer's *Odyssey*—surely one of the central stories that has shaped our culture—Odysseus makes sacrifices to the spirits of the underworld and meets his anima in the form of his dead mother. He wishes to hug her and take her back to the real world, but he can't do that. Instead, what he has to learn from her is to listen to her wisdom, not discount it, as so many men in that male-dominated society would have. One of the great lessons for Odysseus is to learn how to treat women with respect; it's not until he has done so that he's fit to return to Ithaca and to his wife Penelope, whom he has effectively abandoned while he goes off on his male pursuits of war and fighting. Athena, the female goddess of war and wisdom, who is, in her armor, certainly a match for any man, is his guide in this. It's significant, since she represents a balance of the sexes in her own person.

Another of the great recurring figures of Greek mythology is also from Homer: Tiresias, the man who became a woman. Odysseus meets the spirit of Tiresias at the same time as he meets his own dead mother. The legends say that Tiresias saw two snakes mating and hit them with his staff. When he did so, he offended the gods and so was struck blind and changed into a woman. In some versions of the legend, he spent seven years as a woman and had children as well. Then eventually he sees another pair of snakes, and this time when he strikes at them (or in some versions, he respects them and leaves them alone) he becomes a man again, now endowed with the gift of prophecy and eventually revered for his wisdom.

The meaning could hardly be clearer: it's only the person who has truly met his opposite—and figuratively become that opposite, living the experience from the other side—who is able to see clearly enough to be wise in the ways of the world. Again and again the task is to achieve compassion through understanding, which requires us to know the animus and anima thoroughly. When we do so, we move into a new relationship with fate, one that relates explicitly to synchronicity. For that is what a prophet is—one who is linked to divine energy and clearly sees the unfolding of divine purpose.

This idea of the seer, the shaman, being both man and woman, is an ancient idea in many cultures, and it serves two symbolic purposes. The first is that it says this person is definitely not the same as the rest of us but has somehow risen beyond categories. The second point is that the way of seeing that the shaman possesses is not circumscribed within one category of "male" thought or "female" thought; it is a combination of both wisdoms that is more than the sum of its parts.

For Tiresias, the extra quality he gains from his travails is the gift of prophecy, and prophecy was a difficult business in Homer's world. Cassandra of Troy was a prophet. All of her predictions came true but, unfortunately, she could never get anyone to believe her. This is an interesting detail, until we see it as a metaphor as well. Troy is a city where women are not listened to, a place where it is acceptable for Paris to bring Helen, a spoil of war whom he has stolen from her husband and who is treated as some sort of sex toy. Indeed, women are simply objects in Troy, so it's not surprising that Cassandra has such a hard time. Implicit in this is that Troy is a place where men and women do not meet with their animus or anima selves, and this personal spiritual emptiness is partly what leads to its destruction. After all, Cassandra is ignored when she foretells that the Wooden Horse is bad news. And we all know what happens after that.

The lessons contained in these stories are pretty clear: Listen to what the animus or anima has to say, because if you don't you will run into disaster, and you will not be in touch with the true current of the world's energy—the source of the wisdom available to seers and oracles.

Other examples of this mythic theme reinforce the point. In a secondary tale about Troy, Criseyde, the daughter of Calchas, has a similar problem—one that has been repeated in many stories through the ages, including Chaucer's masterful long poem, *Troilus and Criseyde* and Shakespeare's *Troilus and Cressida*.

Criseyde, a widow, is left in Troy when her father defects to the Greeks (women get left behind and abandoned in this society). Her father is a seer who knows that Troy will eventually fall. It's the same motif as we've already seen. Back in Troy, Criseyde is courted by Troilus, a Trojan prince. He is desperately in love with her, and she obviously finds him attractive—but she's only too well aware of social issues, such as how she will be seen if their affair becomes known.

Calchas arranges an exchange of prisoners and wants his daughter to come over to his side of the battle lines. He doesn't consult with her; he simply commands her to do as he bids. Moreover, Criseyde has no option but to obey the order since male prisoners are to be exchanged for her. They are seen as more valuable than she, and as we have seen the world of Troy really doesn't value women very highly.

Criseyde leaves Troilus with the utmost reluctance. When she arrives in the Greek camp, she is practically undefended and quickly finds herself in the role of lover to the Greek soldier Diomede. Notice: she is not his wife but his concubine. It's as if she has no choice, and there is no sign her father is going to protect her in any way.

Troilus takes this very personally, of course, convinced he's been betrayed. And he has been; but in a similar circumstance almost anyone would have acted as Criseyde did, we suspect. She hasn't been able to access her courage, just as Troilus hasn't been able to access his understanding of the pressures she's under. He judges her by his male standards, and she doesn't feel she can operate by those rules. She's just trying to survive as best she can.

The story is a tragedy in which we see that the animus and anima have not been revealed for this pair, and they quite literally do not operate out of the same moral awareness. They are merely responsive to the outer expectations of their society, which is engaged in an insane war. Helen of Troy, stolen from her husband, is revered along with her abductor Paris; yet, Troilus and Criseyde's affair is seen as potentially a disgrace. Where are the moral standards?

If we need a modern comparison, we might think of those women who, at the conclusion of the Second World War, and perhaps believing their husbands to be dead, married the soldiers of the occupying forces. People chose their significant others for a variety of reasons, some less noble than others—some for safety, some out of loneliness, and others out of fear. Some genuinely found love that would last their whole lives.

We could bring this comparison even more up to date. Since the fall of the Soviet Union, many people from various countries have been free to travel to the West, where they have met and married people who were their erstwhile cold-war enemies. Some marry for love; others marry to escape their past and the hardships of their lives. They find a "good enough" partner and settle down. In each case, they are looking for a better life, not a rigid adherence to some sort of national label. If the better life fails to materialize, sometimes the romance fades, too. These are the types of unions entered into by those operating in the ego mind-set. Material comfort is the primary consideration; the heart is hardly engaged at all.

And yet this sort of behavior is a time-honored pattern. I'm reminded of the boatloads of British women who sailed on P&O ocean liners to India in the 1920s and 1930s. They were offered cheap fares because it was more or less overtly understood that they would only be traveling one way—to find a husband in the British-run Indian civil services or military. These marriages were sometimes very happy, and often very convenient. In terms of what we've been looking at, however, these were the marriages that would struggle to find significant spiritual content.

The point is this: under such circumstances, it can be very hard for men to access their more tender anima and for women to lay claim to their animus effectively. The prerequisite in each case is real trust and affection, and the willingness to change and learn from the other person. It can't be easy to do that in an arranged marriage with a relative stranger, or in a circumstance where one's behavior is being forced to conform to strict social guidelines. In fact, it's a pretty sure-fire recipe for the descent into the unconscious to be delayed indefinitely.

Where men and women meet and relate to each other in a circumstance that is too heavily controlled, and where the roles are so rigidly defined, it's hard to do the necessary introspection. If we return to Shakespeare for a moment, his romantic comedies appealed to his contemporaries because the plays presented exactly the sort of circumstances that so many men and women longed for but so few actually got: a real relationship that was based on give and take and mutual self-actualization. No wonder people loved his plays. No wonder so many still do.

The Cost of Not Going Deep

So let's spell this out. The literature has a profound message: those who do not access their animus or anima lead lives that are ultimately emotionally sterile.

A second point also needs to be emphasized here: there are some aspects of personal development that clearly cannot be done alone. One cannot go to a hermitage in the woods and successfully relate to one's animus or anima. One can do other things in such seclusion, but not this. What one learns about the opposite side of oneself has to be lived, every day, with other people. There are other ways to learn this than in romantic relationships. For example, a person doing good work with a therapist can go a long way toward embracing the animus or anima. The main point is that the lessons learned cannot be learned in isolation; they have to be taken back into the world of everyday relationships, with all their untidiness and confusions.

The third point is that in order to do this work, we need to be in a relationship that has some mutual affection in it already, sufficient for each person to feel safe. Some of the people I work with and counsel seem to think that they can refine their personal skills and their awareness of their psyche, until, like a newly painted car, they are absolutely sparkling and in excellent shape. Then they feel they will be ready to go out and find connection. They've done the work, now it's time to test-drive the result.

Well, that may be a lovely comparison, but it's a false one. One pieces oneself together, one grows one's psyche, while being with others who are part of that process. They have to be part of the messy business, part of the painting and assembly of this vehicle. When the vehicle is ready to drive, it's not "my" vehicle or "your" vehicle—it's the vehicle you and I will both be part of. One cannot perfect oneself and then appear, like a grandee at a state occasion (to give another simile), expecting everyone to flock forward and be able to recognize one's inner qualities. That may be a delightful fantasy, but life doesn't work like that.

In my work with private clients, I find again and again that some people think they can't be in any sort of relationship because they're too much of a mess, or not ready, or they are afraid others will look down on them if they reveal their confusions and doubts. These are real fears. On the whole, individuals do need to sort themselves out to some extent before they can have a successful relationship; yet, such fears can erect an unacknowledged barrier, a mind frame that states, *Only when I'm sorted out will I be ready to face the world.*

The trouble is that no one is ever completely sorted out, and it is usually the people who are with us as we try and work on important things about ourselves who are the people with whom we can truly forge relationships. That's one reason people who have been in groups together, or been through difficult circumstances together, are often bonded more strongly than others. Working with others—imperfect, annoying, confused as we may all be—allows us to access an important emotion: unconditional love. That is what is symbolized by the Virgin Birth in which the child is the focus. The child loves unconditionally—the mother, also.

In the everyday world, we love the people we love despite their faults, which allows us to move toward unconditional love. Achieving it fully, though, may take some time and effort. We can dislike people and still love them, if we know how and have practiced the skill. This is an aspect of unconditional love, where we accept people exactly as they are, now. When we do that we've accepted ourselves unconditionally, faults and all.

When we go into the deep psyche we discover that we are all pretty much the same. This makes it hard to hate anyone, since if we are all the same what is there to hate? Hurting someone else would make about as much sense as wishing to hurt one's own hand or foot. We are all one.

Knowing that we are all linked is not a task that we can achieve just by thinking it. We have to feel it in our hearts. We have to work every day to remind ourselves that those people who drive us crazy are exactly the same as we are, because we can be pretty sure that there's someone out there who is driven crazy by us. The story of Jesus is proof that no matter how good you are, someone will be needled by what you do. And then we have to love those people anyway. We have to live this information each and every day, and it's hard work.

The myths and literature are clear: If we can reach this point of self-acceptance, we'll be fully in the flow of synchronous guidance, and miracles will seem to happen all around us. It's a tall order, though.

Summary

To some extent, we all understand that we have to construct a self, a persona, that allows us to face the world and fit in. This need for a social identity is natural. Yet we also have to remember that this self is not the totality of who we are, since we are those aspects of ourselves we've had to suppress, too. At certain points, if we do not remember this, the repressed self will burst out like Sticky Hair, and we have to adjust to this.

Mythology and literature show us that this process is entirely normal and healthy. By accepting this suppressed side of ourselves, we are placing ourselves alongside Odysseus and Dante and countless others, proving that no matter how exalted one is, the work still has to be done.

We undertake this work of meeting the Shadow Self not just to be happy and successful or to get a better job, but because doing so brings us into alignment with a world that is about more than just surface. We are given the chance to find our animus or anima and realize that it can show us the true nature of real love, for that is who we are, each of us, at our core. This knowledge brings us to an acceptance of the eternal struggle of all people, everywhere. It becomes impossible not to love your neighbor, not to care about ecology and the planet, because we see we are all inextricably linked.

The Shadow may show itself as various self-serving actions, but it is at its core a fear of death—a fear that we are cosmically insignificant, totally irrelevant, and that our life is only marginally better than nonbeing. Its chaotic and destructive aspect is simply a reaction to the haunting fear that nothing matters. The power of myth is that it lets us know that we are not alone in feeling this way, and that we are part of something that has meaning. For love doesn't mean anything if we aren't aware of the threat of death that makes it so very precious, and we cannot feel the full power of love until we have recognized its helplessness.

The descent into the self invites us to see ourselves in a new way since it strips us to our core essence. When we know who we are, at the deepest level, then we know what we have to offer, and how to use it without the ego taking over. The ego doesn't cease to exist; it simply functions differently as we use it to remind us of our personal authenticity. It can then tell us how best to use our skills in our lives in order to participate fully in the world, and do what needs to be done for the greater good. The ego, tamed by a fuller awareness of what love is, ceases to be a restless seeker after toys and thrills and starts to be a force that directs each of us in how to act according to our strengths—and everyone has different strengths. Used properly, the ego brings us into the present moment in full awareness. In its new role, it responds to those flashes of intuition and understanding in which we know far more than we thought we knew about a person, or a situation; and it now guides us in seeing what needs to be done. If the energy of the Universe is the blazing light of the sun, then the ego is now the solar panel that can convert that energy into useful action.

This is where synchronicity begins to reveal itself most fully.

Part Two
The Obstacles to Synchronicity

CHAPTER 10

Mind Traps and How We Construct Reality

The Words We Use

Now that we have an overview of how we can move into harmony with the synchronous nature of the Universe, and the things it will require of us, we will need to think more closely about what can get in our way. The mystic Eileen Caddy, co-founder of The Findhorn Community in Scotland, puts it best when she says:

> Darkness cannot be cleared until it has been revealed, brought
> to the surface and seen for what it is. In the light, it has no power
> and will eventually die away to nothingness. [1]

This is echoed by Virgil's Aeneas, who descends to the underworld and is told by the ghost of his father Anchises that he has a task to do: he must found the city of Rome. He is also given advice so that he can "avoid or face each trial" he will encounter along the way. [2] Most barriers to doing what we need to do come from within our own minds. It's as well to be prepared.

We all have mental traps that can ensnare us. We've already identified one: the sense that we have to be ready or perfect before we can begin real life. This is akin to what we learned as children, that we can't do things until someone or something is ready, or until we've been tidied up, or had our hair brushed. *Now you're ready* is the thought.

It's the same mind-set that says that the only important thing is to study for tests and exams, and that when we're told to start we'll be ready, primed, complete. We believe this will make us popular, or better than others. Anyone who believes that is missing a lot of life. We form relationships with people, not with exam results or diplomas. This is one of the most misleading images that people have of themselves. It's the same sort of thinking that prompts us to buy a car or a large expensive consumer durable, thinking that when we have it, *then* we will be happy. We save up for a vacation, *then* we'll be relaxed. We get a spouse and a house, *then* we'll have achieved our dreams.

We think like this because our whole society is structured around that rigid order. We work hard now in order to reap the benefits later. And often we do. But we can also enjoy the now and not worry too much about the later. If we are to free ourselves in order to be in the flow, we'll have to let go of this "now-followed-by-then" way of thinking. Instead, we'll have to get used to the continuous "now." If we're always looking to the future, we'll be unable to see the synchronicities around us... right now.

So let's backtrack a moment. How exactly did we humans get into thinking in this future-oriented way? Well, it may have been part of our survival code. If we got our food and shelter organized today, *then* tomorrow would be easier. If we put things in order while the weather was warm, *then* winter wouldn't be so hard and fewer of us would die.

These are useful mind-sets, obviously. But when we take them just one short step farther, we stop being able to live in the present moment and live mostly in the future—and that's when we lose sight of what matters. The teachings of yoga and meditation are always asking us to refer back to the here and now. Almost everyone will tell you that meditation is hard work at first. It takes practice and effort. This is a clue to how deep and how powerful our attitudes can be. We have far more experience in letting our minds run wild over future possibilities or remembering past grief than we have of letting it all go and being content with where we are.

There are plenty of these hidden mind-traps—habits of mind that lie so deep within us that we aren't even fully aware of how they operate. And if we aren't aware of them, then how can we make sure we don't fall victim to them?

Take, for example, the difference between the way humans and other animals physically see things in their environment. Certain types of birds, antelopes, and other animals have eyes that look out sideways from their heads, giving them the ability to see what is going on around them and even behind them. They can't easily see what lies in front of their noses, and they feel for their food in ways that would seem to us rather less than satisfactory. Because they are always on the alert for something that may creep up behind them and turn them into food, their thinking is going to be very different from ours. We can't know for certain what they think, but we can be sure that we, as creatures with eyes that look forward, tend to look ahead, tend to see what we do see very clearly in stereoscopic vision that allows us to assess exactly how far away something is and what it's doing.

Is it any surprise, then, that this fact of physical ability has tended to mean that we humans "look ahead" in our planning, that we reward those with "focus," "foresight," and "vision?" We value those aspects of sight and seeing that we can identify physically. We ask people, "Do you see?" or "See what I mean?" when we make a point to them in spoken words they definitely cannot see. When we do this, we are reflecting our subliminal prejudices; we even say something is "on the horizon" of our lives. I'm sure you can find dozens more examples.

The clichés we use are entirely related to the physical accident of our bodies. But when it comes to inner processes, we have to use phrases like "internal wisdom" to differentiate it from the more ordinary, outer-oriented wisdom. We talk about "inner knowledge" and "insight"—and the lack of specific words for these inner processes lets us know that we're not as familiar with them as we might wish, and not that comfortable with them, either.

Our very language, the terms we use every day, lets us know that inner awareness is not something we naturally do that well. This even extends to such words as prayer. The word "prayer" derives from a word that had to do with asking for something, as in the somewhat ancient form we still hear today, "Pray consider the following request." Yet prayer can be many things. We can ask the Divine Force for things and actions, we can plead for intercessions, or—and this is the rarest use of prayer—we can use the action of praying to remain quiet and to receive words for our guidance.

Most people still think that prayer is for asking God to do something, rather than for us to listen to what God has to tell us—*Please God, look after the earthquake victims. Please God, punish our enemies. Please God, give us victory.* But these are active demands, not the receptivity of listening for answers. We really don't have much of a vocabulary for this action of listening to the Divine Force, although a growing number of people use meditation for this. Unfortunately, meditation is not as common as one might hope. It reflects an overall paucity of understanding of the nature of our relationship to the eternal. Many times, people I've met have said they prayed for something and it didn't happen, so they gave up on God. These words have come from Ivy League grads and school dropouts alike.

If we are to experience the rich inner life we desire, we may have to recognize that the language we use—the very building blocks that help us construct our thoughts and concepts—may at times be less than helpful in getting us where we wish to go.

Here's another example. A woman asked popular spiritual advisor Deepak Chopra how she could live a spiritual life, raise her five children, and keep her job. She hardly had any time to meditate, she said. How could she possibly have a spiritual life? Dr. Chopra suggested that she could put her meditation first, then everything else would arrange itself around the results. By meditating first she would be much more efficient in everything she did, he said.[3]

It's a neat answer, and it feels true. Certainly, it's counterintuitive. Perhaps the woman was hoping for some hints as to how to meditate more efficiently, or how to find a shortcut. Yet the way she phrased her question was such that it seemed the meditation practice was the problem because it wouldn't fit into her other life.

As we all know, the way one asks a question often determines what the answer will be. Here's a question I might well ask myself: "Shall I rush around and get my things together, finish writing this page, jump in the car, and scurry down for a quick 15 minutes at the gym, or should I sit here, relax, and watch TV?" I think you can see that the way I've phrased it makes the TV option seem much more appealing, even if there's nothing on TV at this time of day. So I weigh the scales unfairly in the way I ask the question.

An alternative response to the question the woman with five children posed might be to ask why she felt she had to "do it all?" Was there another way? Could she arrange to do less work and spend more time with her children and her meditation? Could she organize the children so that they were able to help each other with various tasks that she normally had to do? Could she invite her children to meditate with her? And I'm sure we could make more suggestions if we knew the situation and its details a little better.

The language we choose to use in our self-talk will shape how we see our world, and sometimes we see hopeless situations when there are plenty of opportunities. The woman saw her situation as a problem that had to be solved, rather than as a decision point as to what she was going to place first in her life. She seemed to think that she really could "have it all." This is a common delusion, one that is fostered by advertising media. For example, ads tell us we can have a huge car, which is also gas efficient (so we can feel good about having a huge car), and still afford the payment plan because "no down-payment is required." Well, of course you can afford that! The problem may be that even if you are given credit you actually may not be able to afford the car in the long run.

I'm sure you see the pattern. I suspect that this woman with the five children was a good-hearted and indeed noble mother, but she was asking for advice because the world of "should" and "ought" had got in her way. She *ought* to be able to do it all, she had been led to believe, and to admit that this was not reasonable was too difficult for her.

If we really want to encounter synchronicity and flow, we may want to be aware that going with the flow of events may well involve adjusting our lives in ways that don't meet with others' approval. We can't simultaneously live that life and the life that will meet with universal applause. We may have to make choices.

Like this woman, we all have a tendency to talk ourselves into believing something that is not accurate; yet, at a certain level we are not fooled by words unless we agree to be. Some people are highly skilled in this. Police detectives are very good at assessing when someone is lying—far better than most juries, it would seem. Most of us focus on the words, not on observing nonverbal cues.

So, what happens when we don't focus on the words?

Here's an example. Next time you're in a public space like an airport or a train station, or any place where people travel, take a look around. You'll have no trouble identifying those people who are lovers. It doesn't matter what race or age they are, you'll notice something in their rapport, and it doesn't have to be because they're kissing and nuzzling up to each other.

If you keep looking, you'll see who is bound to whom by other bonds of love. Perhaps, for example, you'll notice how mothers and children interact, even if they're not exactly happy with each other, even if they're tired and bored. When we are at a party and see people flirting, we know they're flirting even from the other side of the room (and even if they deny it later). We see the movements and the facial expressions, and we know what's going on independent of the words. And when we meet someone who is unusual, someone who is perhaps very wise or holy or deeply loving, we remember what it felt like to be near them much more than we remember the words they said.

It may seem obvious when I put it like this. But it isn't. We observe how people are with each other and draw conclusions. I mention this simply because it reflects an inner knowing that is pre-verbal, and which we can be persuaded to discount—if we allow it. The husband may convince his wife by using the right words that he really wasn't flirting with the other woman, but the wife may still feel a creeping doubt, no matter how good the words sound, or how persuasive they are . . .

All of which is to say that we know more than we think we do, and we create our own barriers to understanding, very often, by using words. We're faced, then, with a language problem. There seems to be one language that assures success in the material world of things and acquisitive behavior, and a totally different language that has to do with inner peace.

In the best-selling book and video series, *The Secret*, we are asked to consider that the Universe is a source of unlimited gifts, and that what we need to do is to focus upon what we want and then it will manifest itself to us. This is a true statement. I have witnessed it sufficiently often to be able to assert this. We can manifest anything we wish if we focus on it and ask. Why then, do so many people feel disappointed when they try to use the law of attraction and what they want does not appear?

The problem lies in what we ask for, since we tend to ask in terms of the words and expectations of our society, and this may actually prevent us from getting what we need, although we do get what we ask for. We've already looked at this briefly, but it's worth considering again in detail.

Take the man who said that if he could just get a job that paid $80,000 a year, then he'd feel safe. He was articulating a real wish. Sure enough, after a while he really did get the job that paid the salary he asked for. But he wasn't happy because he didn't really like the job, it took up too much of his life, and he didn't feel safe because he was afraid he'd be fired in the next economic downturn. For this man, the solution was actually alarmingly simple. He'd asked for the wrong things, and they'd appeared.

If he'd started in a different mind-set, one less dominated by the clichés of our society, he might have asked himself what he really wanted more of in his life. The answer was, he wanted to feel safe, and the job and money were his way of articulating that. Had he concentrated on the issue of feeling safe he might have had to ask what safety meant for him. What would it actually feel like, not in terms of cash in the bank, but in terms of how he'd feel each morning when he got up? What would his life need to feel like so he could experience safety? Perhaps he'd need to do some real work on himself so that his fear level decreased? Well, he didn't do that, neither did he even think it was worth doing. He focused on the money.

For many people, feeling safe is not about money but about whether they feel loved and appreciated, or whether they can walk outside with pleasure, enjoying the trees and flowers. If this man wanted safety, then he'd need to sort out what that truly meant for him, and only for him; he'd have to discard other people's ideas about what security is. My insurance agent is convinced I can't feel secure unless I buy a lot of life insurance for my family to enjoy when I die. If I believe his version of reality, I'll buy the policy.

Security can't be bought. It can't be achieved by having "the safest car on the road" with the "best crash-test ratings." It can't be handed to us. We have to find it for ourselves, inside our souls. We have to step away from the words of our society and find words of our own choice that correspond to realities we believe.

Returning to *The Secret* and the Laws of Attraction, then, we have to be careful what we ask for, as author Rhonda Byrne points out. Some people decide that what they want to attract into their lives is more love, and they want a soul mate. This is a worthy ambition, but once again, we have to be careful what we ask for. If we are slightly lost and confused and uncertain about our lives, then our soul mate will almost certainly be someone who is an equal match for us in terms of where we are in our development—in other words, slightly lost and confused. Like attracts like, so we will attract someone who, when he or she appears, may seem like a huge disappointment because this person is exactly like us, and we already know that we're disappointed with ourselves. People the world over truly are manifesting exactly what they ask for, then rejecting what turns up because they have asked for the wrong thing.

In Patti Smith's memoir, *Just Kids*, she recounts her life in New York from the time of her meeting with photographer Robert Mapplethorpe and she describes the way their lives intertwine until his death. It's eerily clear, right from the start, that these two share something very unusual. They understand each other in a visceral way. It's obvious that they are soul mates, but it's equally obvious that they will not be able to make a life together (even though they never seem to separate fully). They are connected, but not in the conventional ways of ordinary couples in tidy homes with kids and a dog.

The whole book is intensely moving and is, in part, a redefinition of the idea of soul connection. The book succeeds because it shows how these two were always present for each other. Each was the other's muse, and each was profoundly creative and experimental. Over the years they grew together in their creativity and their vision, finding more in themselves than they could have imagined. Here were soul mates, but there was no Hollywood happy ending to their story.

The Universe may give you a soul mate, too. But if you want a soul mate who is also a lover and a support and a companion for life, then make sure you envision that and ask for it. We attract exactly what we ask for. In the words of Wayne Dyer, "You do not attract what you want; you attract what you are." [4]

> **EXERCISE:** What do you want more of in your life? What do you want less of? What do you really want? Start by writing at the top of a page, "What I want more of in my life." When you have your list, ask: Will this bring me what I want? On another page write, "What I want less of," and when you've filled that page you can take a third sheet of paper and begin to think about the third question: "What do I really want?"

As you do this exercise, you may be surprised by how quickly you get beyond the accepted, driven-by-the-advertising industry answers. If you wrote that you need a new BMW car in your life, you may decide that it is, in fact, what you want. Perhaps you feel it will make you feel good and important. That may work for you, but it won't work for most people. For most of us, the page will fill with abstract nouns like Peace, Tranquility, Joy, Friendship, and so on.

But the second part of the question matters, too. Will these things bring you what you want? If you look at your list you may decide that worthy as these items are, you don't actually want them as much as you want to make a difference in someone's life, so you can feel you are contributing to the world. Some people think they want peace and quiet, to retire and play golf, when what they really want is to be engaged in life in a different way. It's the difference between "what I want to have" and "what I want to do."

When you write about what you want less of in your life, you're likely to list things like money worries, anxiety, uncertainty, disrespect, and so on. In this list, you'll be telling yourself an important truth: you'll be listing the things you're not going to pay so much attention to anymore. You intend to let them go, so they won't be issues in your life anymore. After all, you made them into issues. You have written this list in order to let go and make space for the things you *do* want in your life. These good things can't appear because there's no space for them—not until you chuck out the old stuff. For instance, I know of a young man who is confined to a wheelchair, and he does not let it get in his way at all. When asked about it he simply says he doesn't make it an issue in his life, so it isn't one. He can't pretend the wheelchair isn't there; it is. Yet he can make sure it isn't anything that gets in his way.

When you find yourself plagued by difficulties, just gaze at your list of things you do want. You'll recognize that you don't want this new problem in your world, either. Add it to the other list, and you can let it go and stop thinking about it. If the first list of things you want more of in your life has many abstract and intangible things on it, such as Peace and Happiness, then the list of things you want less of in your life is very likely to have some concrete items on it, as well, such as bosses who are idiots, cars that break down, annoying neighbors, and so on. Recognize these as areas of stress and resolve to pay less attention to them, or work to remove them from your life.

Remember: the task here is to raise your awareness so that you don't attract more of the things that trouble you.

The list of things you *really* want is the one to treasure. Tape it up somewhere (the fridge is a good place) and turn it into a vision board, if you wish, with pictures stuck onto it, or add drawings (drawing are especially good, even though they take time). Then make sure you look at it, really look at it, every day. Doing this will remind you of what's essential, and it will keep your eyes open for what you actually do want. This list will tend to be midway between the other two, for it will probably include things like more time with the kids, more family time, more movies-and-a-pizza with friends. This list is both practical and linked directly to the intangible pleasures of being with people you love and having fun. These are actual things you can do right now.

If you choose to focus on this list, it will remove the natural tendency to worry. Worry is focusing on what we don't want to the detriment of our wellbeing, to the point when we can only see worry and none of the good things. It's like a man who doesn't like the color of his house and grumbles about it until he can't see the aspects of his home that he does value. Habitually, we blind ourselves to what's good by insisting on seeing what isn't good, or by thinking that the good things are way out of reach. It's time to change that.

Remind yourself to make space to look for and appreciate life's pleasures. When you write out a shopping list or a to-do list, include a reminder to yourself. It's easy. It can be something like, "make sure to go past the house with the beautiful trees on the way to the store" or "run this errand when the rain stops, so it's fun." These are little things, sure, but they add up. You will find yourself beginning to live the values that you want in your life, and as that happens you attract more of them. Remember always: you attract who *you* are.

So let's look at how we attract things into our lives.

> **EXERCISE:** I do an exercise in some of my writing classes in which I ask people to imagine receiving a fortune cookie and reading the fortune inside. What would you like to see on that little slip of paper? Write down a couple of possible fortunes. You can do this now. When you've done that, imagine a fortune that you'd like your father to receive. Now, how about your mother? Your sibling? Write them all down. You can have more than one for each person. Now, how about for a significant other? Write that one down, too.

The fortunes we write down for others can be hilarious; more importantly, they often convey messages the writer wants to send someone but doesn't feel will be believed unless it comes from a neutral source. The young man who wrote asking his father to give up drinking since it was killing the whole family knew with utter clarity that his father would never be able to hear this if he said it straight to him. It was a strong, sad example of how messages sometimes can't be delivered to the correct recipient. Writing it allowed the man to realize it wasn't his fault, nor was it his responsibility, if this message could not be heard by the one person who most needed to hear it. In this way we can free ourselves from self-blame about other people's behavior. We can't change them. Only they can.

At the end of the exercise, I ask people to imagine getting a free toy in a cereal box. What would it be? And then I ask: if you ran the cereal company, and you were in charge of putting the toys in the box, what would the toy or prize be? Finally I ask: if money were no object, what would you place in the package?

Take a moment to do this. Write out the answers, now. I know you want to skip over this, but write it out anyway.

I've been doing this exercise in groups for many years now, and the results are often eye-opening. The exercise is important for a number of reasons. What emerges, I've observed, is that there are some things we long to say to others, that they really won't hear, or that we're shy of saying. The number of times I've seen people write messages to their parents that have said things like "Take time for yourself" or "Just accept how much your family loves you" or "It's time to take a vacation and do what you want"—well, it would break anyone's heart. Loving messages don't get heard; ones that are critical, too, sometimes can't be delivered.

As we go through the exercise, I ask the writers to consider whether they take their own advice. Do you leave time for yourself, too? Do you allow others to tell you they love and value you? Surprisingly often the advice we give others, even when it's good, is also advice we need to hear for ourselves. This is a prime example of the kind of mind-trap I've been trying to show you. We give advice, and because it's good advice we assume that we're living it, too. And very often we aren't—not even slightly.

At this point, it's useful to circle back to the first of the fortunes—the ones we wrote for ourselves. Very often these are statements like, "All your waiting will be rewarded" or "Hard work pays off." Pretty clearly, these are hopes for a positive outcome for situations that are as yet uncertain. We want to be reassured that things will turn out the way we expect. Of course we do. Yet only we can truly reassure ourselves of anything. If I say to someone, "Everything will turn out fine," perhaps that person will look at me and say, "How do you know?" That would be only reasonable.

These initial fortunes are useful, therefore, in identifying the ego hopes we have. These are the things we may have to let go of. Simultaneously, if we realize that we need reassurance, we'd better take steps to be the one offering it to ourselves and remember to act with courage. Those initial fortunes remind us that our hopes are only hopes, that we may have cope without them, and that the only approval that matters is the approval we give ourselves.

The responses to the cereal package part of the exercise tend to be either very practical or very fanciful indeed. The person who included a small package of hope and joy in every box of cereal was thinking differently from the person who wanted a really reliable and long-lasting watch to plop into the breakfast dish. Many people say they want to receive the keys to a new car (often a specific type), or a million dollars. Others ask for happiness, or world peace. Obviously, there's a difference. In each case, though, the question has to be: What are we doing to achieve these goals? Items like this rarely drop into one's lap. What are we doing to bring this about? This sometimes awakens the realization in group members that they have been, at times,

strangely passive when it comes to making their lives happen. Often we want someone to provide these things for us, as if we had a fairy godmother. And that attitude
has to change.

When we arrive at the part of the exercise that has to do with what we'd give out
as gifts if money were no object, the responses are also often extremely varied. The
question I ask in return is: How generous were you with others? Were you able to
give freely and believe in abundance, or were you worried the imaginary cereal company might go broke? If this were a real company, then the practical considerations
would matter, but the exercise specifically uses the word "if." Were you able to go into
the imaginative space or did you stay in the practical? For the notion that lies behind
this is alarmingly simple: the way we treat others is the way we tend to treat ourselves.
The way we love others is directly related to the ways we love ourselves. Were you able
to be generous to others, or not? And just how generous are you to yourself? Do you,
in fact, love yourself? And is generosity merely a question of money and jewels and
toys, or is it something else?

These are difficult questions to face, but they are vital.

The center of the exercise is, as you may have guessed, that it gets everyone concerned pondering their luck. We all believe we have luck, even if we believe in nothing
else. Some people believe they only have bad luck. There's a 1960's Cream song, "Born
Under a Bad Sign," whose lyrics go: "If I didn't have real bad luck, I wouldn't have no
luck at all." [4] Obviously it's a blues number, so it has a slightly gloomy edge to it.

Your luck will be about as good as you believe it to be. If you believe you're cursed
or unfortunate, you're buying into a self-image that may have nothing to do with the
world or reality. It's time to examine your self-image, the one reflected in this exercise, because it could be one that you may not even be consciously aware you have.
It's also time to be aware of the words you use and how they affect who you think you
are. Then you have to throw out the negative thoughts that don't serve you. How else
will you get in the flow?

CHAPTER 11

Struggling Against Flow and Destiny in Literature

Oedipus, Jesus, and Jonah

My wife, Cat Bennett, is a skillful leader of art and drawing groups, as well as a published author. In her book, *The Confident Creative*, she uses drawing exercises to awaken readers to the possibility of being in the flow. [1] The first thing she tries to do is to get her students to let go of "doing it right," since in art there is no right or wrong way. When we let go of wanting to be right, we let go of all those voices that surround us that tell us how a picture "ought" to look. Unfortunately for us, we've internalized those voices, and we've started to believe them. Perhaps we've believed them for many years, since kindergarten, when we were told our picture wasn't as good as Billy's. As Cat will tell you, it takes a while to break away from this, but when we do then real creativity floods in.

So take Cat's advice and let go of judgment.

In one of her exercises, she has her group do a drawing and then she asks them to tear it up. Mostly they are aghast. Tear it up? But I worked so hard on it! Shouldn't I be preserving it? The point she makes, which I want to emphasize here, is that we don't have to become overly attached to what we create, because if we do we'll block our flow of creativity. If we can rip something up, feeling confident that more good creative energy will come, we're actually trusting our own creativity. And that allows it to come even faster. We have dozens of pictures inside us, waiting to emerge. Don't attach to any specific one just yet, or even at all.

It's a little harder to do this with writers, but I say the same thing to my students. Writer Anne Lamott says something very similar in her book, *Bird by Bird*, when she states that we must allow ourselves to write "really shitty first drafts." [2] Write it down, and be prepared to accept that in it is some small thing that may be useful; or perhaps not.

When I'm working with writers, we sometimes reach a point at which a section has to be rethought or rewritten. There's a tendency with some writers to fiddle with what's on the page in the hope of getting it "right." Often the best advice I can give them is, start over. Usually the second draft, composed when the first has been destroyed, so it can't be used as reference, is far superior in every way.

If you doubt you have an unending source of creative energy, you'll only be able to access a very small amount of creativity. When we think that there's only a limited amount of flow available to us, and that we must save every ounce of it, we're just cramping our own style. To stay in the flow, please do not cling to everything you do. Have the faith to start over if it feels like the right thing to do.

Burt Munro, the eccentric motorcycle engineer whose story was the subject of the movie, *The World's Fastest Indian*, had a shelf in his workshop with pieces of broken and twisted motorcycle engines that had destroyed themselves in speed attempts. He placed a sign above this shelf of mangled alloy that read: "Offerings to the Gods of Speed." [3] The reminder, one that he saw every day, was that we try, we sometimes fail, and it doesn't matter, because we learn and try again, and there is no limit to our creativity.

Burt is a good example of what we are talking about here because he took his ancient 1920 Indian Scout motorcycle and turned it into the fastest Indian motorcycle in the world. He did it because this was what he really wanted to do. Even if this is something that doesn't appeal to us, we can still learn from it. Flow is available to everyone, not just writers and artists and athletes and people who wish to learn about how to live a spiritual life. It's freely available.

Think of it this way: a politician rises to prominence offering change and greater equality. He or she has charisma and is in the flow. Things go well for this person, and soon he or she is acclaimed as a new president or leader. The challenge at this point is to stay in the flow and not force things, any things, faster than they can be realistically accomplished. Unfortunately, history is full of such figures who tried to make things happen, became impatient, and who were seen as tyrants. Some truly became tyrants because they wanted to consolidate their position and focused on that, rather than what the country needed. Think of Charles Taylor, the former charismatic president of Liberia, who is presently awaiting trial for war crimes.

By contrast, consider former South African president Nelson Mandela, who rose on a wave of massive support and, through judicious leadership skills, was able to avoid a war between the South African whites and blacks—a war that most people thought was inevitable. After his first term was over, Mandela stepped down. He could easily have won a second term, so great was his personal popularity. But he didn't even try, and his gesture sent a profound message far and wide. In an Africa that has seen far too many dictators, he was signaling that the new South Africa was going to be about people sharing power, handing on the responsibilities to others. The next wave of politicians would be trusted to stay in that place of willing service, not of ego.

This is a message about staying in the flow. It is not about you or me or Nelson Mandela; it is about what flows through us all, if we choose to pay attention to it, and it is bigger than we are. We are its servants.

When we see that flow is about us being, in some ways, subservient to it, we reshape our awareness of what is going on. Inspirations that come from the place of flow are to be paid attention to. Once again, mythologist Joseph Campbell is very wise about this, and throughout his work names it "the call." When the call arrives, he says, we ought to pay attention to it, "because it may not come again." That's a rather more pressing thought. [4]

I've worked with some writers and memoirists who have felt that they had missed their first call to become writers or actors or musicians because they were afraid to follow it. Their fears were usually to do with money or family expectations. For some, the call really didn't come again, and they have written with regret about what they feel they missed. The call was an invitation to move closer to the divine creative spirit that is at the center of the Universe. It may not ever repeat itself. Yet not all is lost. Think of it as like being invited to a party. Perhaps you think about it and decide to stay home. Or perhaps you only hesitate and arrive late. Or possibly you only go when a friend calls you and asks why you're not there. Finally, you go. It won't be as much fun that way, but you'll still be part of things. There are many ways forward.

The call may be to the creative life or it may be to serve our fellow humans, but what is important in each case is that we give up the attempt to control things. That comes from our imagined dominance in the physical world of the ego. We think we're in charge. We think we're in control. But how much do we truly control? Turn on your TV and watch the victims of the latest disaster—an earthquake, perhaps, a train wreck, a tidal wave. How much control did those people actually have? Very little. The only thing we can control is our reaction to such things. We can regulate the way we feel and the way we shape our lives afterward. That's all. This may sound frightening, but it's only a cause of fear if we wish to interpret it that way. Instead, it could be seen as a reminder that there is a flow, one that is bigger than we are.

This is not the same as being helpless, though. That is the familiar response of the black-or-white thinker who says: If I'm not in control, then it must all be beyond my control. This is logically flawed, as I'm sure you can see. What we have to try and establish is how much control or input we actually have. Where do we stand on that continuum between passivity and total control?

Short of having a hotline to the Almighty, it'll be hard to discover this. How much control does a bird have over the air currents? Not much. But it learns how to use them.

We may once more need to get some help from literature and legend. Literature has always been a way for people to uncover insights about themselves and learn more. Carlos Ruiz Zafor puts this elegantly when he has one of his characters say:

> A story is a letter the author writes to himself to tell himself
> things he would be unable to discover otherwise. [5]

It's often only when we try to write or explain things for someone else that we find out what's important and valuable in what we have to say. We discover our meanings in trying to express them. For the reader the process is roughly similar, according to science fiction writer Ursula Le Guin:

> We read books to find out who we are. What other people,
> real or imaginary, do and think and feel is an essential guide
> to our understanding of what we ourselves are and may become. [6]

Let's take a look at some renditions of this specific problem of fate that people have felt to be true over the course of centuries. They could give us hints as to the way fate operates in our lives. What we find will turn out to be remarkably consistent.

In classical Greece, society was viewed as being made up of human beings and above them a pantheon of gods and goddesses who lived on Mount Olympus and were as likely to make disastrous mistakes as anyone else. They meddled and entangled themselves with human affairs and fought and squabbled over the results. Independent of the Olympians were the prophets and the oracles whose prophecies could not be avoided, not even by the gods who were subject to the same forces of fate as human beings. As a result, when Greek statesmen and kings wanted guidance they first visited the oracles at places like Delphi, rather than just praying to the gods. There was a sense of a large, powerful immutable fate, and of a lesser, more localized fate that could be altered by prayer.

The most striking example of someone caught up in this sense of destiny may be Oedipus to whom, as we may well remember, fate is especially cruel. He thinks that fortune has smiled on him, making him King of Thebes. However, years before, the oracle had announced to his father that Oedipus would marry his mother and kill his father. Horrified by this, his father had taken steps to have Oedipus killed; he did not know that the baby had been rescued by a shepherd from the hillside where he had been left to die. When Oedipus grows up he hears a prophecy that he will kill his father and marry his mother. He doesn't know that he's been adopted. So he runs away from what he believes to be his family—and straight into the fulfillment of the prophecy. It can't be avoided.

Within the Christian tradition we have a similar series of ideas. Even Jesus, the son of God, could not escape his destiny on the cross. So there seems to be a divine order that is more powerful than anything else. This is echoed in such Biblical stories as Jonah and the Whale.[7] Jonah is told by God to go to Nineveh. He rebels against the idea and goes to Jaffa and then takes a ship for Tarshish. While he's on board the ship a storm arises, and the crew discover through casting lots that it's Jonah's fault. Since Jonah admits he is disobeying God, and the crew cannot get the ship to shore, as a last resort they take Jonah's advice and throw him overboard to calm the storm. He's then swallowed by a whale. He spends three days in the whale, and it vomits him up on the seashore, right in front of Nineveh, exactly where God had told him to go.

The obvious point here is that one can't rebel against God, or fate. The next part of the story is even more interesting, but it's the part most people forget about. When Jonah is in Nineveh, God makes him prophesy that "in forty days Nineveh shall be overthrown." The effect of his words is so strongly felt that everyone decides to fast and pray to God to spare them. Even the king is in sackcloth and ashes, praying for deliverance. Seeing this, God decides to spare the city and its inhabitants. And what is Jonah's reaction? He's upset that God hasn't kept to the absolute letter of the prophecy, and he goes into the desert and sulks. Nineveh has been "overthrown," just not in the way Jonah imagined.

When we see the whole story in this way, we can appreciate it as a complete meditation on the way fate works, and how God's will can occur in ways that may surprise us. Once the city of Nineveh repents, God has no need to destroy it, so why should anyone cling to the letter of the prophecy—especially as it's only Jonah's literal interpretation? The city has indeed been "overthrown," but not by fire. Fate has been fulfilled, but not in the expected fashion.

If we see this episode as history (which is unlikely since no one survives being swallowed by large sea creatures), then all we have is a strange tale. But if we see it as a metaphor for how God or destiny operate, it may actually have something to tell us.

In fact, this short tale is full of meaning in the way it shows events turning out in ways that do not flatter the ego of the individuals involved. Think of the followers of Jesus who expected "The Kingdom of Heaven" to appear and were disappointed when they didn't get a complete political reshuffle that conveniently put them at the top. The mocking note nailed to the cross, "Jesus of Nazareth, King of the Jews" (usually depicted as its Latin shorthand, INRI) shows that what people expected was not the same as what they got. Yet the world was changed, as we know. Jonah wants the word of God to work the way he imagines it ought to, literally and as stated; instead, it works the way it needs to. The detail of Jonah spending three days in the belly of the whale is a pretty strong hint that we should make this connection to the three days Jesus lay dead and buried after the crucifixion. Fate, it seems to say, is not here to serve our ego-gratification, but to move larger processes forward. But—and this is important—we can only see this if we read the story of Jonah as a metaphor, and see it in its entirety rather than just looking at the first half.

This is one of the most difficult things for people to understand today, and it is still problematic when it comes to religion. Probably the majority of people worldwide read their chosen holy texts and treat what is said as literal truth. In fact, as we can only be too well aware, many of the texts are metaphorical. The creation of the world in six days and the Garden of Eden are not important as facts; they are important as metaphors that allow us to apprehend what lies behind them, and we would be well advised to consider them as one way of exploring our relationship to the divine.

I write this knowing full well that there is a Creation Museum in Petersburg, Kentucky, that purports to show the literal truth of the Bible, complete with dioramas that display Adam and Eve, discreetly veiled by vegetation, as they actually were in the Garden of Eden a mere 6,000 years ago, as the curators claim. That's all very well. But it restricts our understandings greatly if we chose to accept this rigid point of view. It places a specific interpretation of a text before us in such a way that we are not allowed to question it. It replaces spirituality with religious dogma. The viewer is asked to accept and become passive—not to think, or feel, or wonder. We may also want to bear this in mind when we consider such places as 'The Holy Land Experience' theme park in Orlando, Florida, which advertises all Bible re-enactments and activities, all day.[8]

Currently there is considerable discussion of the year 2012, which is to be, according to the Mayan calendar, the end of this world. This is an interesting idea. Yet what if this is not a fact but a metaphor? What if 2012 turns out to be a time when there will be a spiritual shift that amounts to the same thing as an end to the established ways of doing things? If the end of the world is a fact, then it triggers one set of responses; if it is a metaphor, then it will cause entirely other reactions. Indeed, as a metaphor it could be deeply inspiring, encouraging voices that might have been silent until now to speak out and be part of the change.

Myth, legend, holy script, and literature are probably our most reliable indicators of how we can look at this topic of fate, but we cannot afford to become rigid in how we consider it.

The discussion of fate has never been easy, but it has often been described with great emotion. Let's consider Hamlet, the most famous fictional figure in western literature—possibly in all literature. The story of Hamlet is well known. He is told by a ghost, which he believes to be his father's, that he must revenge his father's murder. The murderer is his uncle, who has now married his mother, taken the throne, and made Prince Hamlet stay in Denmark under virtual house arrest. What is he to do? That is, of course, the question he wrestles with in the celebrated "To be or not to be?" soliloquy. He doesn't find any answers; in fact, the more he thinks about it, the more questions he has.

But Hamlet's problem is, once again, not only the situation but also how he formulates the questions he asks. Which action should he take: A or B? Kill Claudius or kill himself? Each way leads to certain death. Commit suicide and you go to Hell—at least as far as seventeenth-century belief was concerned. Kill the king and the chances of being caught are practically a certainty, so it's as good as suicide. This is a no-win situation. Yet, at no point does Hamlet pause and say to himself: *I don't have to do anything yet.* Instead, he thrashes around, feigning madness, perhaps actually slipping into madness, and he sets off a string of reactions that kills everyone of note, including himself. By the end of the play, everyone who has been involved in the action is dead, so the kingdom is cleansed and everyone gets his or her just desserts, even Hamlet. After all, he'd killed Polonius, so his reward is death. Justice is served for all, one might say.

Seen in a different light, though, one could say the play is a consideration of fate and destiny, and that Hamlet's problem is he tries to fight against fate. He thinks, at least at first, he has to take control. If the play has a message for us, it could be that fate will come to whatever conclusion it needs to. It's like saying that the train of destiny will travel along a certain track and will reach its end, but as passengers on the train we have the choice of how we behave. We can turn the trip into a hell if we wish (which is what Hamlet chooses), or we can opt to behave well and trust that fate will turn its karmic wheel to where it needs to be.

In our time, we've seen repressive and evil regimes collapse from the inside (think of the former Soviet Union and its satellite states). We know that evil has a way of crumbling in upon itself. The trouble is that while we wait for it to do so, millions of people suffer. So, is patience a virtue or a lost opportunity? The Dalai Lama says, repeatedly, that nonviolence is the only way, and it's a message that was endorsed by Mahatma Gandhi, Dr. Martin Luther King, Jr., Nelson Mandela, Jesus Christ, Moses, and others.

I'd like to suggest that nonviolence is almost certainly the best way, and it does not mean doing nothing. Instead, it means allowing ourselves to be part of the flow so that we are nonviolent yet still connected to the creative, generative energy of the Universe. We are not immobile; we are motivated by a different series of values, ones that require just as much energy as rebellion and resistance.

By the end of the play, Hamlet has accepted this very different point of view. He puts himself in the hands of fate. "There is a Divinity that shapes our ends, rough-hew them how we will," [9] he declares, accepting that whatever comes will be perfect. That's good Buddhism, although I doubt Shakespeare knew what Buddhism was.

Now, this is a viewpoint that will have many challenges. Should we not have re-acted to the 9/11 terrorism attacks? Should we have simply engaged in creative tasks instead?

Again, there is no easy answer here, no either/or option. The question, once more, seems to force the response. Perhaps we could observe that we chose, as a nation, to put events into action over the previous 40 or 50 years that led, eventually, to the rise of the kind of terrorism that we are presently struggling to contain. To some extent, we were participants in a process that caused some dangerous people to become far more dangerous, far more angry than they already were, and we didn't listen to them. Now they won't listen to us, either.

If we focus simply on one major historic event that precipitated a violent re-sponse, such as the 9/11 terror attacks, or the Japanese bombing of Pearl Harbor, or the sinking of the *Lusitania*, or the assassination of Archduke Ferdinand, then we are distorting our understanding of these things. Those events were the end result of a series of events that led up to them. We cannot pretend otherwise. The desire for revenge is very natural, but it's a desire to put right something that was going wrong long before the event that triggered the response.

The lesson we can draw from this is one we can take back into our lives. The partner who leaves us or betrays us doesn't do it out of the blue. It's always the result of a long series of previous actions and discontents that weren't getting articulated in any other way, so a decisive action takes place that means we can't fail to pay atten-tion to the situation any more. The exact same thing is true of almost everything we can think of. The teenager who becomes destructive or out of control is in essence no different.

The lesson for us is that destiny is all too real. Since we cannot predict what spe-cific course it will take, we have to make sure that we work toward being the best people we can be as we feel our world moving toward that destiny. Think of it this way: we are born, and we know we will die; in between, we can choose how we live. We can choose to respect others and grow more love and peace. Or we can choose to disrespect others and ourselves and create the opposite. We can mistreat our bodies by eating too much or drinking too much, and shorten our lives in the process. But this will not alter the overall destiny of the planet. The most horrible evil-doers have a way of causing others, in reaction, to become more compassionate, more brave, and selfless. As countless others witness positive examples, they too are moved to emulate them. Evil has a way of creating good, even when it doesn't want to. That, too, is the nature of flow.

Ultimately, we do hit some sort of wall because, as mere human beings, we simply cannot see far enough ahead to be able to judge definitively how fate works. And that is important, for if we definitely knew the outcome we would not have freedom of choice as to how we are going to handle the here and now. We'd be constrained by the end result we knew we were headed toward.

What seems to echo throughout literature and myth, though, is a sense that evil does not triumph for very long, and that fate makes things turn out the way they need to, even if at the time it may not look like they can be resolved. Is this is just a consoling sop that we need in order to get through each day? It could be. It could also be a deliberately constructed belief, formulated by the dominant powers throughout history as a way to keep the huddled masses from complaining too much. This seems less likely. Nations have, certainly, constructed national myths to rally populations, but on the whole these have faded quickly. They've been too crude either to have any real imaginative resonance for most people, or to feel true for very long. One way or another, we keep coming back to this basic optimism—this trust that fate will take us somewhere and that we have to be part of that process.

When we recognize this, when we give up our ego-world of control and personal achievement, we agree to listen to what's happening and be part of the flow of syn-chronicity. Perhaps the existence of flow is the subjective experience that proves to us that there really is a larger force in the Universe than just us. Those who haven't ever ventured into this flow won't know what we're talking about, and they won't believe us. How can they? How can they know, first hand, that sense of some force guiding us in little or great things, the gentle nudge that tells us to pick up this idea and write about it, or to create art this way, or any number of irrational but productive impuls-es. For those who have never felt inspiration, there are only practical considerations. For the rest of us, there's flow.

CHAPTER 12

Refusing the Flow

The Role of the Heart

We can all choose to refuse to acknowledge fate or destiny. To return to Hamlet, he could, possibly, have just decided to go along with his uncle's immoral takeover of the kingdom, be thoroughly complicit in it, and have had an easy, wealthy life as a result. He could have been a collaborator, just as many people were when the Nazis came to power in Europe, for example. This would have been the most disgraceful form of opportunism. It would also have been a refusal to respond out of the best part of his awareness. But the call comes to Hamlet, and he feels he has to do something. As we've seen, he responds in the least helpful way. What he doesn't understand is that standing to one side, out of the current of evil, is not the same as refusing the call to action. Sometimes it's the only thing we can do, at least for a while.

We all have the choice to refuse to act from our own best and most vital center. In one of my workshops was a man who had just retired at 70. He had been an engineer, and he said to me that he'd always wanted to write poetry, but he hadn't done so since he was 22 years old. Now he wanted to start.

Well, I didn't want to be discouraging, but in the intervening years he'd written hardly a line and he'd read even less. Worse still was that when we spoke he had no idea what, if anything, he wanted to say. He loved words; that was clear. It was also clear that he'd chosen the safe life of a good job and regular raises rather than the unsafe way of actually pursuing the activity he loved. The trouble is that poetry can't be picked up just because you like it. And just as the body fades, so does the ability of the brain to take on new tasks. For example, at that age he could not have become a truly excellent athlete. He'd simply left it too late. And as for writing, it takes time to refine the craft. Keats famously said that he knew he'd have to write four thousand lines of an extended poem (*Endymion* was the result) before he would be able to come into his true abilities as a poet. This older gentleman didn't have the time, and he hadn't kept up the practice. I tried to be encouraging, but soon we both knew he'd let his dream slip away.

This failure to act is all the more surprising because the Universe has a way of sending us the same lessons over and over until we get them right. So one could say that these opportunities never fade. To take just one example, any parent knows that if you don't set up a few basic understandings when the child is very small, then the resultant confusion in the child's mind simply breaks out more powerfully when the child gets older. So then you have another opportunity to set the necessary boundaries. And if that doesn't happen, then the child pushes the limits and you get another opportunity.

I've seen this first hand. The toddler who learns he can get away with anything because the parents don't enforce limits will grow into a pre-teen who believes that the rules don't apply to him or her. If the parents don't respond to this, or to the parent-teacher conferences that usually accompany this, then the child really doesn't believe the rules apply to him. And by the teenage years, a young person who doesn't think any of the social agreements and laws have any hold over him is likely to get into all sorts of trouble. Eventually, such people can even wind up in custodial settings, behind bars; and then they may finally get the message. If the parents can't learn, the child suffers too.

In these instances, we could say that the world has provided plentiful and repeated opportunities for change. In exactly the same way, we often receive the heart message as to who we are when we are very young. We know we love drawing or painting or reading or sports from a very young age, and we set off down that path not knowing quite where it may lead us, but we go along and explore happily.

If that ambition does not motivate us, it may call to us again at a later age, and until we are about 15 or 16 years old we'll find it easy enough to respond. But after that age things become a little more complicated. We may have friends who expect us to be a certain sort of person, and taking a different course of action can feel lonely and isolated. As we grow older, we have a job and a boy/girlfriend or a spouse and then there are children and a career, and with each passing year it feels harder to break away and be ourselves. We wind up accepting what others think we should be because our confidence in our own self-determination has been eroded.

When that happens, we're caught, or put more precisely, we've trapped ourselves. When we become our own jailers, it's very hard to get free again. The first process, the life of the unruly child, is essentially not fully conscious. The child is rarely happy running out of control, but has no sense of being able to do much about it. This second process is, by contrast, one in which we do have choices, but our conscious awareness of what the world expects of us overrides who we truly are.

Again, it's a knife edge. We need some parental direction when we're young so our ego does not run out of control. And when we're a little older, we need less control from our ego or from others and more of a sense of what we love to do most. This comes from the heart, but we also need the ego to help us balance our lives so that we can do what we wish, so that we can fulfill our destiny.

The refusal of flow—the missed opportunity for learning—is often easily noticed by those on the outside, while the person who has missed the chance cannot see it at all. Here's a recent example. A student of mine came to see me in tears one day and told me she had been beaten by her boyfriend. We had a long talk, and I advised her to never see this person again and to keep in touch with me so we could see how she was doing.

The very next day she sent me an e-mail to say she wouldn't be in the next class. As it happened, that day an unexpected opportunity arose when a woman from one of my other classes came to address us about abusive relationships, of which she herself was a survivor. It was an intensely moving presentation, and I wished with all my heart that the young woman who was supposed to be there, who was facing this exact problem, could have taken her courage and attended the class. Instead she was at home, sobbing, and making plans to visit her abuser again.

I cannot begin to count the times this sort of thing has happened. Synchronous events are all around us, but we have to open our hearts to what is going on and take the risk of being vulnerable rather than hiding away. Opening the heart is another way of saying that we need to operate from a place that is not ego-based; and feeling like a victim can sometimes be a powerful ego mind set, since it allows us to blame others. As we've already seen, the descent into the self shows us how we can strip away our ego fixations. Once these are gone, we'll see how we, ourselves, helped to bring about the situations we're in. That's when we can learn from them and let them go. Now we need to look at another way forwards, an ascent like Dante's laborious ascent to Heaven, that suggests how we can use our sense of compassion most fully.

The Role of the Heart

One of the best ways of describing this ascent is to refer to the idea of the chakras, a Sanskrit word that means "wheel," referring to the energy centers described in Indian and Ayurvedic medicine, and which are integral to the practice of yoga.

According to this system, there are seven chakras, spread along the length of the body aligned with the spine. In yoga, an ancient practice that literally means "union of mind-body-spirit," the task is to uncoil the chakra serpent energy, the kundalini, which lies sleeping at the base of the spine, and permit it to stretch upward fully, to the top of the head. It's a metaphor—no one thinks there actually is a serpent in our bodies— but it serves as an elegant description.

A study of the chakras in all their complexity would take a book of its own, certainly, since each chakra corresponds to a physical, a mental, an emotional, and a spiritual level of awareness. For our purposes, I wish to sketch out only a general schema of how they function in terms of spiritual progress as the individual's awareness moves upwards through the sequence. Necessarily this will be an incomplete description. What we'll find is the heart chakra is the transformative mid-point in this progression.

The lowest chakra, the first chakra, is at the level of the anus, and it is concerned primarily with the challenges of survival and instincts. Security is important at this level.

The next chakra is below the belly button at the level of the genitals, and has to do with sex and family and our relationships. We all know this one, as sex can become an all-consuming drive for many people, but it also relates to money and creativity and self in relationship to others. Both the first and second chakras relate to belonging and are heavily influenced by external conditions. Spiritually, the second chakra is the center that governs enthusiasm and joy.

The third chakra is the one at the level of the solar plexus, between the sternum and the navel, and this is also concerned with getting and keeping and enjoyment, but instead of focusing simply on the objects of pleasure it is a more general drive towards personal power and growth. All three chakras are, so far, part of what we see in the physical world of getting ahead, making money, building a career, finding a spouse, and so on. They are important, but spiritually limited.

The fourth chakra is that of the heart. The heart is the seat of the emotions, but it can be in service to the lower chakras, those emotions about gain and status, or it can be in service to the higher chakras, in which case the heart has the capacity to open to greater compassion. This sense of feeling for others and being connected to others and to their welfare is very different from the more self-oriented values of getting and holding in order to be accepted by the group, and that is what we see in the first and second chakras. Obviously, we can't have the higher order of being without the ones upon which it stands, so these are all important aspects of who we are.

When the heart begins to open fully, it can show its true power. For above it is the throat chakra, which has to do with the will to express the compassion the heart feels. We don't just feel love; we find we have to express it and tell someone about it. At this level, we trust in love and in the divine power of the universe, rather than in our own striving. This means that the fourth chakra, of the heart, isn't just halfway up the body or halfway through the sequence of seven; it is a symbolic midpoint and a gateway to the higher self that can accept flow. It is the essential point that has to be reached so that we can be fully who we need to be.

The heart chakra appears in various guises in many myths and legends. For example, legend has it the Buddha was born out of his mother's side, close to the heart chakra, and this must surely remind us of Eve, who was born from Adam's side. It's a curious detail. After all, if Adam could be created directly through God's generative wishes, why not Eve? Why this taking out of a rib? The story gestures at a symbolic virgin birth based on equality, and based on the heart.

If we look for other virgin births in other religions, we see them plentifully. We've already observed in Chapter 8 that American Indian myths have many virgin births and that in European myth we have the odd examples of Athena and Dionysus. Dionysus was ripped from his mothers' womb and sewn into Zeus' thigh. Since he emerged in due course to be the god of sexual abandon and ecstatic experience, the thigh, close to the genitals, was therefore a good place for him to reach full term. Athena, the virgin goddess who appeared fully armed from Zeus' head, was a different creature altogether, as one would expect from a goddess born from the head. She was rational and calm and associated with scholarly or warlike pursuits. Exactly what one might expect.

So in Greek myth, we have versions of the virgin birth that come from above and below the heart, as if to suggest the need to balance these qualities out. The boyish and undisciplined Dionysus, who is often naked, is the exact opposite of the upright and orderly virginal young Athena in her armor.

If we shift to Christian iconography, we can add to this the image of Jesus found in practically every church and shrine. This is of him sitting in his mother's lap, at the level of the heart, and occasionally feeding at her breast. We can see this as a representation of the opening of the heart chakra, since he's sitting at the level of the heart. It's a beautifully elegant image, since babies routinely do sit on their mother's laps anyway, so it seems ordinary and mythic at the same time. The mythic shines through the ordinary.

Jesus, of course, was on Earth to open people's hearts, so it's not as if we're stretching the connections here. Which brings us to the question: what does this sort of birth actually convey? We've already looked at this, but we have not pursued its meaning to its fullest extent.

The birth of Jesus, the Virgin Birth, was not a physical fact in the way we understand physical facts. The Catholic Church has had to work hard to make the idea fit the notions we have of the physical world. Instead, it has to be understood as a metaphor. The angel tells Mary she will conceive, and she does, so the message here is that when we contact the transcendent world in our own experience then we become "pregnant" with celestial energy. This happens at the level of the heart. In time, it leads to the rebirth of the self.

As is true of any birth, the mother's previous life does not return to normal afterward, because now everything has changed. She is a mother first and last, and she will never again be simply a private individual. What this says to us is that when we experience a beautiful spiritual moment, then a sequence is set in motion that leads to us being reborn to our notion of who we are and our place in the order of things. At such times, life isn't ever going to be the same again. The Virgin Birth actually is a representation of the opening of the heart chakra, and the changes that then occur.

Have you been awakened to your spiritual nature? That is what it asks us.

Plato refers to this in his *Symposium*, where the priestess Diotima tells Socrates she is "pregnant in soul." It is exactly the same idea.

Once the heart has been opened, then our entire relationship to the world changes. Just as a mother is, like it or not, now the supplier of the next generation's needs, so we can use the metaphor to see that we are here to serve the universe's needs, not our own.

When we understand this, spring is not just a season when we can finally put away our winter boots; it is a rebirth for Earth, this larger life in which we are all participants, and also a spiritual experience, for we see Nature's heart reopening, too. Earth provides us with a new growth of plants, the birds return, there is food available once more. At the same time we can choose to see beyond the mere fact and into the greater cycles of the earth. These cycles of seasons were here long before us and will continue after we're gone. Our bodies will die and decay, and we'll become part of that cycle, new growth emerging from our dust and ashes. Spring therefore reminds us of the mythic order, and of our place within it; this place is not the ego place.

The Christian church used this mythic quality, building on older religions to do so. We have no idea when Jesus was conceived, and his birthday in December is a polite symbolic fiction to do with bringing hope at the winter solstice, when the earth is at its darkest and the nights at their longest. Jesus is born, hope grows, and the days start to get a little longer. And the church was very canny about this, because Lady Day, the feast of the Virgin, nine months before Christmas, is in spring, the time when the world is waking up. This links the Virgin Birth idea firmly to this notion of new stirrings not just in the womb or in Nature, but in the psyche and the spirit.

The heart chakra is, therefore, one of the most important chakras, and in various mythic forms it appears across the world. It is the point at which spiritual rebirth occurs. In Sanskrit, there is a symbol that was later taken over by the Jewish tradition: it is now known as The Star of David, composed of two triangles, one on top of another, one pointing upward and one pointing down. This ancient symbol was originally one that was placed over the heart in pictures and art, and it indicated that at the level of the heart we have a choice, either to go upward with what is new, or to go back down with what is old and follow the way things have always been done. We can accept the call, or refuse it.

This is exactly the heart's dilemma. We can always choose to go back to the way things were in the lower chakras. These chakras, when healthy, take care of vitally important aspects of our lives and we need the balance they provide. The serpent of rising kundalini energy needs every part of itself working harmoniously. And yet, the task of the first three chakras is also to support the upper chakras, so we can move forward into the new, more compassionate space of being reborn to our divine possibilities. We can protect the heart, or we can exercise it more fully.

If we return to the sequence of chakras, what we see is that the fifth chakra, the throat chakra, has the function of expressing, through the voice, the new-found compassion brought into existence in the heart chakra. Above that is the sixth chakra, at the level of the mystical "third eye" between our two eyes. This is the point at which we stop seeing just with our own mortal eyes because we become aware that there is another dimension, the spiritual dimension, which we can see inwardly. This is why Hindus often have a *puja*, or prayer mark, on their foreheads. It indicates that the spiritual chakra of divine insight has been opened. Now, this can't happen if the heart hasn't been opened first. Remember, in the myth the snake has to rise up from the base of the spine.

The seventh chakra, or crown chakra, is on top of the head, and it is symbolic of the connection to the heavens above us. In Indian tradition, it is a portal, a place from which we send out our love and spiritual awareness, and also a reception point through which the energy of the Universe comes into our brains and bodies. It shows the way we interact with the Universe, allowing the energy to flow through us, so that we are aligned with God energy.

Again, none of this can happen if the heart chakra is not open. For our purposes, this way of seeing is a powerful one because it shows us the vital role of the heart, and also that the head is not merely for thinking and calculating but for receiving inspirations and energies that are not of our own creation. How different this is from our habitual way of thinking in the West! It takes us back to the idea we examined earlier that praying is not about asking God for something but perhaps about receiving something from God, because we've stilled the ego for long enough so that we can listen.

Here is Persian poet Rumi once again, who gives us this unusual idea of prayer in his poem "*Love Dogs*," where the same idea is relayed as a dialogue:

> "Why did you stop praising [God]?"
> "Because I've never heard anything back."
> "This longing you express is the return message."[1]

Prayer in this instance is not about getting something back, but about yearning for closeness, which is itself a holy experience.

Now, this concept of the chakras is an actual description of how energy moves in the body. It can also be seen as a metaphor, which is how I have been considering it here. And like all metaphors, it is not the final word on anything, but rather a symbolic map to show us how things may be understood. It is a language for understanding the heart-and-head relationship that we can borrow, learn from, and cherish. Is it a perfectly accurate map? We'll probably never know; yet, we can say that it feels true in many ways, and we see that it has worked for many people for many years.

For our purposes, we need to remember that the heart chakra is the key to understanding at higher levels, one that can bring us into harmony with the energy of the universe, and therefore with synchronicity. If we acknowledge its opening as a turning point, then everything changes. But we can, if we choose, ignore the opening of the heart. That is when we refuse the flow and return our energies to their lower levels.

CHAPTER 13

Getting Yourself in the Flow

The Experience of Bogus Flow

If you've read this far, you probably already know the sense of flow from first-hand experience; but if you haven't felt it for a while, then it's important to re-hearse a few details. Being in the flow means letting go of what you feel you ought to do under a specific circumstance, and keeping your mind open for other ways forward.

Obviously we cannot be foolish about this. Closing our eyes when driving in or-der to let go of control is not a sensible plan of action. Still, most of us experience more flow than we recognize. We go clothes shopping and, because we're not look-ing for anything specifically, we may find the most perfect jacket. If that happens to you, buy the item, even if it's expensive. And if you really can't afford it, do the next best thing, which is to wear it in the shop and enjoy it. You can even take a picture of yourself in the shop's mirror (almost all cell phones have tiny cameras) and revel in the moment. By doing this, you'll be honoring the experience of flow even if you can't take the jacket with you. Send the picture to your friends, take delight in your find. When we honor flow, we get more of it.

I've known many musicians who have done exactly this with instruments in mu-sic shops. They go in, play on a really good piano or guitar, and relish the moments they spend in this way, even if they know they can't buy the instrument, or at least not yet. By enjoying the instruments, they are honoring the music and the experi-ence, not the ownership of the object.

If you want to see flow in action, watch a game of soccer or hockey. Flow is less visible in American football, where the moves are often so carefully planned that there is far less chance for flow situations to emerge over a period of several minutes of play. You'll notice how the players have to be aware of what's going on, who is moving where, and then they have to see if they can be part of the overall movement. These things can't be planned. They happen because of a response that is almost instinctual. The players let go of the precise set plan, and move ahead with what is, with what seems like a good idea at the time.

Staying in the Mind Space of Flow

So let's get practical. How can we make sure we stay in this mind space?

In my book, *Write Your Memoir*, I suggest a number of ways we can train ourselves to be more mindful and bring more peace into our lives. Reflecting on who we are through writing about our experiences has a way of slowing up our responses so that we can be fully aware of what we're choosing. Often we choose things without actually thinking about them. We say things and think things that are not charitable, accurate, or fair, even about those we love—simply because the words jump from our lips so readily and we forget them so fast. Everyone has had the experience of speaking and being interrupted by someone who says, "Can you say that again?" And very often we can't. The words move too swiftly. Writing, and rereading what we write, can change that dynamic, slow us down, and make us more mindful.

Think of mindfulness by comparing it with un-mindfulness. Many stores here in the United States encourage us to take large shopping carts and fill them up. If our shopping carts were a little smaller, and if we had to carry everything instead of wheeling the cart to our cars, we might well think differently about how and what we buy, and how much of it, too. But we are lulled by habit, by recorded music, by all we see, and we become even more cognitively sleepy when we get to the cash register, wave our plastic card and then get cash back if we want it. How wonderful! We buy more than we need and then someone gives us money! Hooray! It's not until weeks later when the credit card bill arrives that we see the true cost of our ways of doing things.

Next time you go to the store try paying in cash. Count out each note, and pocket your change. Feel your wallet getting skinnier. See how differently you'll feel when you're conscious of precisely what you are doing. Like writing things down, this process gives you the chance to think about how you live, and how you choose. The stores that we visit know about this tendency we have, and they work very hard to convince us to spend more, consume more, and think things through less. That's their job. That's how they make money. And they don't care if we slide into debt, suffer, and despair. They still make their money.

They give us an experience of what I call "bogus flow." It offers us the illusion of effortless purchasing.

I'm not suggesting that shopping is evil. I'm simply suggesting that we have to take the time to be aware in our lives, and that means all aspects of our lives, and I use shopping as an example. If we don't pay attention in our lives we'll actually invite in problems where they could easily not have had to become problems at all. The flow can't work for you if you are worried about the consequences of doing something you did while you were on autopilot. You'll simply wind up fighting a system that feels out of control, when really, it was you who allowed yourself to be manipulated into this dangerous situation. As a result, all you'll be able to do is fight or collapse in despair. Be mindful—you'll increase your chances of staying in a place of flow.

The Specific Words We Use

Let's take a moment and look at some other things that can keep us from being in the flow, or perhaps we can see them another way—as things that will drag us into a negative flow.

Let's build on the idea of slowing down our words and paying attention to what we're saying by considering the specific words we use and their appropriateness in a given situation. Using language appropriately is a lifelong skill, of course, and most of the first 12 years of life is about finding reasonably appropriate words for everyday objects and experiences so we can be intelligible. But we must be careful, for it is all too easy to turn a tiny event into a drama. Spilling coffee on their best jacket becomes for some people a major event, a "tragedy" a "disaster," a "huge setback," when it is at worst only an inconvenience or an embarrassment. I'm sure we all know "drama queens"—and "drama kings," too—who turn small events into large ones. Perhaps you do this yourself. If so, ask yourself some questions about it.

First: what advantage are you seeking by creating a drama? There's always an advantage, or we wouldn't do it. Some people make entire careers out of this—think of comedians who turn domestic events into hilarity. I see real genius on TV all the time, and on Facebook, where people comment on tiny things as if they were major events, and the result is hilarious. I say to myself, *I wish I could write like that! It's witty!* And it is. People give pleasure and get praise for doing this, which gives them pleasure, too. And yet, it also can become a thinking habit that will ensure you don't let go of the small stuff.

The balance can be redressed only if we become conscious of the language we use and surround ourselves with, which sometimes we start to believe. If I tell myself that my team not winning the pennant is "the end of the world," I am expressing a disappointment but not a truth. The world has not ended. My world hasn't ended. I'm just sad, that's all.

The problem of inflated language is one that comes to us every day through the media, where news events are built up to be excessively important by enthusiastic presenters. The misuse of the word "tragic" is one example, so that we no longer really know what the word means. To this, we could add words like "disaster," "shocking," "devastation," "horrific," and so on. If everything is a drama, then how do we value anything?

Now, you may think this is a minor point, but I'd disagree. Many Americans today do not know what they are feeling, and it's really hard to know how to exist in the world if you don't know what you feel. So creating drama is, for some people, a huge relief, because then they *do* know what they're feeling—in this instance, they're feeling a strange mixture of angry, hopeless, annoyed, and slightly depressed that *this always happens to me.* Notice that. Nothing "always happens" to you, with the possible exception of the bodily processes of breathing and blood circulation and so on. Those vital processes, incidentally, are unlikely to be things we'll complain about— we'd only complain if they became difficult and didn't "always" happen.

So take a quick look at these two statements:

This always happens to me
What does that really mean? Am I truly under some sort of curse?

I knew it would happen like this
Can that be true? Did you have a prophetic sense of this that you ignored? Why?

Can you see how these might be familiar statements that can lead us into some unusually unproductive thinking? In each case, simple disappointment has turned into a major issue or complaint about the nature of reality.

Buddhist thought makes this point elegantly. The heart of the four Noble Truths Buddha taught is that all misery comes from the wrong perception of reality. Echoing this across the centuries might be Shakespeare's Hamlet, who famously stated that, "There is nothing either good or bad, but thinking makes it so." [1] Since so much of our thinking occurs in language, and language is always a little imprecise, we must be extremely alert to what we say. We can make our realities anything we like because we believe our own words about what those realities are. Put another way: Be careful you don't believe your own publicity.

This impacts us directly because the sources that we use to form opinions about our lives are often less than reliable. The television and news media run polls that regularly tell us what we think and what we approve. We hear the percentages and are either upset or vindicated. We are, in fact, being told in very crude terms how we are feeling. You're either happy with the way the President is performing, or you're not. There is little tolerance for subtlety of thought or for being in the middle ground. We don't want or need someone we don't know to tell us how we are feeling. Yet the news anchor will report that "consumer confidence" was down by 65 percent, or Wall Street lost 100 points, or that 30 percent of Americans disapprove of the way something or other is going. This is not just reporting; this is powerfully persuasive, subliminal manipulation that has the effect of making us restless, upset, angry, and sad—and disempowered.

In many of my classes and discussions, people say that there's always bad news on the television and radio, and they find it depressing. What is the world coming to, they ask? I can't say what the world is coming to, but I can tell these people to turn off their TVs and radios, and observe first hand how the world actually is. Constant bombardment with bad news is inevitably depressing, and it can make us physically stressed and even ill. We know this. This is not the first time this has been said. But we still go back to watch the news and wonder why there's no good news, or so little of it.

There are many people who will say that this is part of a conspiracy to make the voting populace apathetic. I'm not a conspiracy fan, personally, but I can see that this sort of exposure to negative language has a poor effect on human happiness. It also helps sell pharmaceutical drugs. Antidepressants are now prescribed to one in every ten Americans, and one in four will seek medication at some point in their lives. Others self-medicate with legal and illegal substances at a rate too difficult to determine.

Things don't get any easier when we look at the knock-on effect of such attitudes. Stressed and unhappy people do not treat each other lovingly. Anxious and over-worked parents and teachers say things to children—their own and other people's—that are hurtful and that the children internalize. They then believe these internalized messages. *I'm useless at everything—Mom says so all the time. My teacher tells me I'll never pass the exam. Our school is the worst in the whole of Boston. We live in a bad neighborhood. These people are mean.* With messages like this going around one's head is it any surprise that we have unruly schools and troubled neighborhoods filled with crime?

There is talk—how we describe ourselves on a day-to-day basis, usually based on observation. Then there's self-talk—how others describe us, and our choice to believe this view of ourselves as true. This self-talk may originally have come from parents, teachers, our local social arrangements, lawmakers, the media, the government. Self-talk eventually takes over from talk as the source of what we feel is true.

Neither of these may be right or accurate.

Talk depends upon many things. Put sentient beings in poor physical circumstances—overcrowded, with not enough love and constant criticism—and the message they will draw is that the world is not a pleasant place. If this is the usual circumstance in which someone lives what do you think will be the result? We call it the ghetto and wonder why the people in it are so troubled.

> **EXERCISE:** Here is what you can do to counter this. Write a
> brief narrative of your day. Print it out double spaced. Now go
> back to it, and look for any negative statements. Did you use the
> word "not?" Could you alter it? Could you change "Lunch was
> not bad" to "Lunch was okay?" Write it in colored pen or pencil.
> Blue is good, so is green; red is not always so good—it reminds
> too many people of term papers with critical comments and er-
> rors pointed out. Look for any pleasant things in your day. Did a
> friend talk with you? Did you share a joke with a co-worker? Can
> you write about that in terms that are pleasant? If the bus came
> on time, include that the bus came on time and that this was
> welcome.
>
> When you're finished read through the whole description
> and cross out the negative statements so you can replace them
> with positive ones. Then type it up and print it out. Read it
> again... slowly. Can you feel a difference?

One woman I worked with found, to her astonishment, that almost all her statements were negatives. She had developed a habit of saying, "It's not that I'm cautious" or "I'm not the sort of person who..." and any number of variations on that theme. There was hardly a positive statement in anything she wrote. Seeing how often she did this set off some alarm bells in her mind.

In response to this exercise, some people find themselves saying something like, "Positive statements are all very well, but . . . " I call this the "yes, but . . ." trap. When someone uses this statement, it's their way of politely telling you they've stopped listening. "I like your idea, but... " translates as, *I hate your idea, period.* "That's all very well, but... " translates as, *No, it isn't well at all, whatever it is, and you, the person who thinks it is well, are an idiot.* Watch for this phraseology. It's a way for people, including ourselves, to stay negative. Try for a moment replacing "but" with "and." Feel the difference?

This exercise may seem rather basic, but I have to tell you that when I've used it with clients, sometimes over the course of several weeks, things begin to change.

People see that there is joy in their lives—probably more than they thought—if only because they took the time to identify it. Often I call this practicing gratitude, since that is what it is. It's a powerful way to break those verbally based mental habits that keep us thrashing around in the minutiae of life and prevent us from ever discovering flow in any form whatsoever.

If you do this exercise a few times and truly can't find anything worth valuing in your day, then I'd suggest it is high time to change your employment, your place of residence, or your entire life. In fact, almost any change will do, since this life arrangement clearly has nothing at all to offer you. Sometimes, when I suggest this to people their reply is, "Yes, but... ," and that tells me right away what I need to know. They like being unhappy. They prefer it.

That's a real choice, and it has to be honored. It also has to be pointed out to the person concerned that he or she is choosing this path, and other choices are available. "Ah yes, but you don't understand..." will often be the reply. The same pattern re-emerges. Often it is not me who misunderstands. The one who doesn't understand or doesn't want to understand is the one who is rejecting all the offers of assistance, and the phrasing of the rejection suggests that I am the person who is inadequate. I'm the one who "doesn't understand," so obviously I'm the one with the problem. This is our old friend the blame game, and it achieves nothing. If we can blame someone else, we exonerate ourselves. It's an easy dodge.

A variant on this exercise is what I call the "Not Me" narrative. The task is simple: to write a day in the life of someone who is your polar opposite. Most people grumble at this, then fairly quickly they start to enjoy writing about someone who is rude to the boss, or who doesn't do what's expected. In fact, most people start laughing at the mere notion that the person who is "Not Me" can do these things. Laughter is good. Laughing at the things you habitually do in order to fit in is also good. Being aware of your own chains is important. It helps you to break free of them.

So, do you recognize aspects of yourself in any of these things?

Let's look again at the language you use. How about a few other statements, such as "I ought to" and "I should?" If you use these types of constructions, ask yourself who's going to punish you if you don't do the things you ought to? The answer is often you are the one doing the punishing. "I have to do housework" may sound true, but it's the harshest way of describing the action. Try saying, "I chose to do homework/housework/laundry/and so forth because this will have long-term advantages for me, and life will be easier." It then becomes a gift you give yourself. Do you see the difference? "I'd like to do x, y and z" suggests that this is a healthy choice, taken on because the actions produce positive effects.

Now, compare it to the more victimized "I've got to do x, y and z... " If we use constructions like "got to," "have to," "ought to," and so on, we're actually telling ourselves that this is a burden we dislike and don't respect very much. This dramatically reduces the chances of our enjoying doing these things or doing them well. And if we don't do them we'll simply reinforce our sense that they weren't worth doing. In this way, we beat ourselves up before, during, and after the task. That's a three-game loss where it could have been a match-winning game.

There are many such word traps to watch out for, but I'll just mention a couple more. One is the way we tend to say "I believe" and "I know" and use them as if they were logically valid points. You may believe what you like, but that does not mean you are right. President George W. Bush was extremely good at saying that he "believed" something to be the case, and that "we know" that something else was the case. Sometimes, as in the war with Iraq, there was no evidence at all to back up certain assertions, such as claims of Weapons of Mass Destruction (WMDs). But George Bush still "knew," and acted accordingly.

Ask yourself how you "know" what you know, and whether your "beliefs" are always productive. Consider, for example, the statement: "I know the boss/administration won't take any notice of this... " This could be a true statement, or it could be untrue. Yet many people use it as an excuse for not doing something before it has even been considered carefully. I've used it myself. Here's another one: "I know that boy is out there getting into trouble... " It may be possible to know this for sure if one is psychic, but it could just as easily be untrue. All it is, then, is an unpleasant judgment that conveys the message that the speaker expects to have an unruly child and feels that this is the only possible attitude.

When we think like this we allow ourselves to slip into the mind's ready-made boxes of prejudice, and these are often very unfair to ourselves and to others. We permit ourselves to think in clichés, and so we cannot think intelligently or compassionately about what the way ahead might look like. Do not believe everything you think; and think, carefully, about what you believe.

Perhaps John Lennon put it best when he wrote, "People say I'm crazy... well, I tell them there's no problem, only solutions."[2] Of course there are problems, but by focusing on the problematic aspect we can lose sight of the real joy of finding possible solutions—and never find any solutions at all. Where will you choose to focus? Watch your language and you can shift your awareness.

CHAPTER 14

Expect Help Along the Way

When we connect with the energy of the Universe, when synchronous events help us along, we can see this as us joining a helping pattern that's as old as human legend itself. In practically every legend, from the earliest times onward, when the main figure sets out on the path toward the destination that will result in self-discovery, various helper figures appear along the way. Some are good, and some are bad. It's a pattern we see in *The Odyssey*, when Odysseus encounters both kind and hurtful figures. Think of Circe, or the Cyclops, Nausicaa, and Calypso.

It's a theme that echoes down the centuries. In the Grimm brothers' fairy tales, some of which are very ancient in origin, and in many other folk tales, when the main character sets off along the road to fulfill a quest, small figures appear. Often these are dwarfs, or odd sprites, or strange animals. If they are treated correctly, and with respect, they agree to help. This motif appears so often that it's part of the expectation the reader brings to all such tales.

In many ways, this is exactly what happens when we're in tune with our real destiny. Synchronicities happen, doors open, opportunities appear. The point about these helper figures is that they do three things. First, they help the hero. Second, in doing so, they reassure him or her that he or she is on the correct path. The third aspect is even more important. These figures only help those who treat them with love and respect. Synchronicities function that way. They tell us we're not wasting our time, even if our friends and relatives have other plans for us and try to argue otherwise: the challenge is not to be stubborn or arrogant as one goes on one's chosen life path.

But as we have seen with Circe and the Cyclops, there is a negative aspect. In the fairy tale known as *Little Red-Cap* or *Little Red Riding Hood*, for example, the apparent "helper" is a wolf who is not considering the girl's best interests. [1] Her task is to remain firmly on the path her parents and elders have told her she should cleave to. This seems to go against the general sense of finding one's own path—it seems to tell young women to obey at all costs. We need to look a little closer than this interpretation allows, or we will miss the point of this tale.

Pretty clearly the wolf is a form of sexual temptation—the scene in the bedroom would seem to suggest that—and he represents the older man (a wolf by any other name) who wishes to prey on young girls. The tale is important because it opens up the discussion about those people who pop into our lives who are intent on hurting us. They may appear just as miraculously as any of the benevolent and curious figures in the other tales, and they may be hard to identify. Think of the hairy man in the tale *Iron John* who turns out to be extremely helpful but hardly an easy character to deal with. He's every bit as scary as any wolf.

Yet this is exactly the point. When we are following someone else's plan for what we must do, as Little Red-Cap is, then we can be led astray because the task is not fully our own; we lack that inner sense of firmness that causes us to reject what is not helpful. At the wolf's suggestion, Little Red-Cap goes off to pick flowers, as we recall, and so the wolf is able to get ahead of her to her grandmother's house. The hint seems clear: Red-Cap doesn't fully understand her mission; she thinks it's about going to grandmother's house, when it's actually about whether she can protect herself, wherever she goes. When we're on our own path, we know right away what and who is helpful. We cannot be fooled for long. Our inner sense of authenticity won't allow us to be waylaid without giving us plentiful promptings.

In the fairy tale, Little Red-Cap has to be cut out of the wolf's belly after she's been swallowed. She is "born again" and is wiser this time. From now on, she will follow her own inner knowledge based in experience. The tale speaks to us about finding our own authentic reasons for being on the path we choose.

How, then, can we be sure we are on the right path, and not straying like Little Red-Cap? How can we be true to our inner guidance? It's actually rather straightforward. The most powerful of these inner promptings is genuine happiness. If we feel real joy in every step we take, then this is our psyche reassuring us that, yes, we're on the right path, no matter how difficult it may be sometimes.

If the joy drains out of whatever it is we do, then this is important information. Is the loss temporary? Or is it part of something else, something that has settled in for a good long time? The task is to get back to the joy. Little Red-Cap may be gathering flowers for her grandmother, supposedly, and that's all very nice—but the tale tells us she gathers flowers until "she remembered her grandmother." She realizes she's been diverted. It's that shock of recognition that lets her know she's been doing something that is not part of her task, even if it seemed like a neat idea at the time. Clearly, this is not just a tale designed to keep children obedient; it is a comment on how we can misdirect our energies for "good" reasons that are thinly disguised selfish reasons.

When we notice this it comes with a feeling of shock, sadness, and guilt.

Little Red-Cap is just one of a whole series of tales that have to do with helping figures who are, in fact, figures who test the main character. These are familiar features in many tales. Think of the wicked queen who tempts Snow-White with lace stays, combs, and apples in *Little Snow-White*. The ego desire for what is attractive is what leads these figures astray. Unless we have a very clear idea of the path we have to follow—which Red-Cap does not, at least at first—we'll lose our way.

In practical terms, this sort of situation happens every day. The purity of intent we bring to what we do can be subverted by others. For one artist friend of mine, this emerged when his book on art was a great success and a publicist came along to help him spread the word. With the publicist came a consultant who simply wanted to make money out of the venture, and who did not care about what my artist friend wanted to convey about creativity and freedom. It was this person who caused my friend to feel that his lifework had been hijacked. He became less and less happy with what was happening, and only regained his sense of joy when he asked the consultant to leave the team. He'd had a close brush with that pressure to sell out that so many of us face when we are authentically ourselves. He knew something was wrong, because it made him feel unhappy. The joy had, temporarily, drained out of his work.

I could add further examples, but they would all be very similar in their overall shape.

This may be at the root of the Dalai Lama's advice to us that our task as human beings is to be happy, *no matter what* (my emphasis), and even if there seem to be more attractive options easily within grasp. This is similar to Joseph Campbell's advice to "Follow your bliss." Note he says "your bliss"—not someone else's. As Howard Thurman writes: "Ask what makes you come alive, and go do it. Because what the world needs is people who have come alive." [2]

Coming fully awake like this allows us to reach through the temporal and contact the eternal, the transcendent. It allows us a way out of our usual dimension of what we do everyday and puts us in touch with something multidimensional and much harder to explain. We break through to something bigger.

When I tell my memoir-writing students to follow the energy of their writing, and to go where it takes them next, I'm saying the same thing. Let go of the ego, which plans and wants the story to go one particular way (the way that they think will appeal to the *New York Times Review of Books*, usually), and listen to the heart, for the heart has its own ways. When they do this, these writers achieve substantial amounts of joy—and not the joy of getting a good advance from a publisher, necessarily. They get the joy of knowing that their work matters to their souls, that it is vitally alive.

Follow your joy, and you can't miss your destiny. Oprah Winfrey has some useful words to share on this topic, too:

> What made me successful is the ability to surrender my plans, dreams, and goals to a power that's greater than other people and greater than myself. [3]

Who could put it better than that?

CHAPTER 15

Thoughts We Hold that Keep Us from the Flow

Decoding Unconscious Messages

Thoughts and beliefs come from many places, not all of them reasonable or even sane. One of the exercises I have people do is to write down the messages, spoken and unspoken, that they received when they were children.

Take a moment and do that now: what were the messages, spoken and unspoken, that you took in as a child?

For example, the child who received hand-me-downs may have "heard" the message that she didn't matter as much as the older kids who had the clothes first. Conversely, if the clothing was from a beloved sibling or a parent, then the child may have felt that this was a real honor to be wearing Bobby's team jacket, or Dad's coat, or Mom's scarf.

Which was true for you? Did your parents expect you to be responsible and give you tasks that required you to demonstrate maturity? And was that something you valued, or was it just a way for them to get you to do things they didn't want to do? Which is true for you? Did you feel looked after, or perhaps you felt too protected? Did you have freedom, or did you feel you were allowed to run wild? Were you the favorite or not? Was this good or bad?

Sometimes parents and teachers have told their children that they could become anything they wanted, and this can be immensely empowering. It can also be felt, in some circumstances, as the pressure of expectation. Some parents would just love their child to become some sort of star, but the child's more authentic choice might be something completely different, and that is where even positive regard can become problematic. The girl who decides to become a policewoman—an actual instance I came across—may not sit well with the father who wants his daughter to become a media personality.

Looking at your life growing up, did you receive the sense that life was going to be hard, or that life was going to be engaging, with real rewards? Was it alright to trust others, or not? Did people stay in your social circle, or did they leave? And if they left was that due to death, divorce, arguments, or other factors? If you haven't already started, take a few minutes now and write down your responses.

It's worth doing this exercise because a surprisingly large number of deep-seated prejudices are formed during childhood, and they may be formed for very good reasons. People may have been unpleasant or destructive around us. This does not necessarily mean that all people will always be that way. Unfortunately, many people believe that "all men leave," "you can't trust anyone," or "you're always better off on your own" as a result of these early impressions. They might have been true then, but they may not be true any more. In fact, as life strategies at that time these may have been life-saving beliefs, but they may not be helpful after one has reached one's twenties.

One woman took this exercise to the next stage and started to add up all the people who had died that she had known or were neighbors when she was a child. These included grandparents, the father of her friend across the way, a neighbor. In total, nine people she knew had died before she had reached the age of 10. The number included adults and children, and at least one suicide. None of this was ever talked about openly. The message the woman received was, therefore, complicated and frightening. It led to her belief that this was not a kindly or stable world—a belief that had shaped her life for the next 40 years, even though it was not a conscious belief.

What we're looking at here is a process in which we all unconsciously invent beliefs for ourselves and then proceed to live them. Some beliefs can be identified in terms of their origins. We may need to ditch some of them when we see they don't apply anymore. For example, in the Sixties we all believed that Japanese products were junk, based on the flood of cheap toys and small domestic products that had a tendency to fall apart. That perception was true then, but it isn't true now. The same thing applies to our life attitudes. We need to know where they came from and whether or not we still can use them productively, or whether they're keeping us stuck in an old pattern. While we're stuck there, firmly in the world of the ego, we won't be able to spend much time thinking about our souls. We certainly won't be able to see synchronous events for what they truly are, either.

Decoding Messages from the Body

A related language is the language of the body. It's fair to say that we listen only to selected parts of what our body is saying to us through its particular language of sensations. We're quick to respond to the desire to rest, eat, and have sex, and we notice pain readily, but for most of us that's about the extent of our willingness to think about our bodies.

Many of us are unable to hear and respect what our body tells us, even if it's degraded in common speech to the level of "gut feelings." Unfortunately, we routinely talk ourselves out of following our gut feelings. So it is, then, that we agree to do all sorts of things that we know aren't a good idea. For example, in a moment of loneliness, we may go back to a lover, despite feeling severe doubts about him or her, and allow our sense of personal inadequacy to overrule the much more helpful guidance of our intuition.

Our bodies are exquisitely sensitized to deal with the outside world and reflect our inner world, yet we overrule the information the body tries to communicate. We blush, we hesitate, and we do a thousand little things that let us know what we are feeling—and we ignore them, for the most part.

Ask yourself a few basic questions. Do you respect your body? Do you pay attention to it when it hurts or just pop painkillers? Do you give yourself good food, sufficient amounts of clean water (not soda), and try to stay away from harmful chemicals? Do you place products and chemicals on your skin and hair in order to look better? Are they benign or harmful? If they are harmful you are sending yourself two messages: the first is that you don't look good enough as you are, and the second is that you can abuse your body in order to offset that imagined deficit. This is seductive thinking.

Every day in my classes, I see young women who, in the middle of a gray winter, have deep tans supplied on a regular basis by tanning salons. Now, their skins may be fine with this, but according to most dermatologists, this dedication to tanning is definitely not a good idea. It can spark cancers and will cause these women to have leathery skin and extra wrinkles in their early forties. But to a 20-year-old, that's too far away to think about. So, do you take care of your body for the long term—or just in order to look good today?

What we need is balance. By all means be good to your body and your skin. Use wholesome products to nourish it, preserve it, and keep it at its best. That's respect.

How you treat your body is a language that signals how you deal with the world. Do you rest when you need to? Do you exercise in order to create a more muscled body or to offset the effects of a sedentary job? Do you wear comfortable shoes and clothes that keep you warm or cool enough? My mother, a housewife in the 1950s, tortured her feet with high-heel shoes and wore clothes that looked good but were not, as it happened, warm enough. She felt her image was more important than discomfort or long-term foot health. So ask yourself: Do you feel delight in your body? Do you treat it well? Are you pleased to have such a vehicle for your soul and psyche? Or do you neglect your needs?

How you feel about clothes can also help you examine your attitudes, whether you are male or female. Do you like good clothes? Or do you feel you have to buy only cheap ones? If you buy cheap clothing, do you have a reason for doing so, such as a fondness for certain styles? Or are you scrimping to get by? Some people buy expensive clothes because they don't like themselves very much and hope to offset this, talking themselves into believing what they can't accept about their attitude to themselves. Other people truly enjoy the textures and the feel of clothes, no matter where they come from, and they find self-expression and joy in wearing interesting combinations of items. The clothes are an expression of joyous fun. Ask yourself how you treat your body in terms of clothes, then see if this reflects an underlying attitude to how you feel about your body. If you don't like what you discover, make changes.

Stereotypically, many men in the part of the world I live in, the northeastern United States, do not seem to care much about clothes. Faded jeans and sweatshirts rule, for the most part. In fact, it would be hard to separate this "male" attribute from a culturally determined ritual based on attitudes about sexual identity. A well-dressed man, in some parts of this country, is automatically assumed to be effeminate or gay. This is the exact reverse of, say, many parts of Italy, where men dress exquisitely for precisely the opposite reason. Clothes reflect many attitudes. Which ones are true of who you are?

Not worrying about bodily comfort may be a sign of a rugged character, a reflection of someone who toughs it out with basic and dull food as he or she engages in the struggle for a successful life. But this, too, is a poetic statement: the individual is expressing that life is a struggle, that one has to be tough, and that there will be a reward for this self-denial. There is nothing wrong with this mind-set—many athletes and explorers have it; however, I'd suggest that it, too, is part of a "story" we tell ourselves about who we are, and it may turn out to be more attractive to hold on to the story than to be at peace with the body.

People who force the body to its limits may well be people who force other things in their lives. When we force, we go against the idea of flow. Forcing means that we tell ourselves that we can make something happen a certain way. That may be okay in some circumstances, but more often, little good comes from this kind of attitude. Like insisting that a child eat all his green beans before being allowed dessert, it may deal with the green beans in the short term, but it does nothing to make the child like them—nor will the child like the person who does this to him or her, setting up problems for later on.

Forcing is a way of getting something "done" in the least effective way possible. That's why flow is never something that can be applied through sheer willpower. Do you force your body to do more than it can do? Do you rest when you have the flu or battle ahead anyway? And what about your bed? Is it comfortable? Do you sleep well in it? Do you allow yourself enough sleep and relaxation time?

The question about your bed may seem a little personal, but I have noticed alarmingly often how many people have mattresses and beds they don't like and aren't comfortable sleeping on. The result is more back pain, more aches and pains of all kinds, less sleep, more fatigue, and eventually this leads to depression. Our bodies will usually cooperate delightfully if we treat them decently. Yet we so often don't.

This whole question of the body has to do with our increasing estrangement from the physical world we inhabit. Not so many generations ago, most people got up with the sun and went to sleep when it went down. We don't do that now, and there isn't a soul I've spoken to who actually enjoys getting up in the dark on a winter's morning. What a way to start the day! We are out of rhythm with the days and the seasons. We're also out of rhythm with the world of physical work. We have cars to take us everywhere, so we don't walk. We have wheeled shopping carts for our shopping, so we don't carry what we buy and feel its true weight. We get on elevators, and so on.

Car culture is the sort of culture that has people driving to the gym, when they could walk and get the exercise. It also has helped to keep us unaware of bodies in general. In the days of horses, one had to feed and care for the animal that pulled the cart in which one sat. We got used to having to do this so the horse wouldn't die. A car makes no such requirements. We can put in a tank of gas in two minutes, leave the car out in the rain, and change the oil only when we feel like it. Some people treat their own bodies this way. Food is to be consumed in several gulps as energy shakes or nutritional bars. What happened to chewing with enjoyment, savoring the food, and giving our bodies that treat of pleasure—or at least a leisurely meal?

When we do these things, we are sending ourselves messages about what is important in our lives. These messages are all the more persuasive because they are not fully articulated to us. We are saying that life is not about being present, enjoying where we are now; instead, life is about making sure we're not late for the next big thing, looking good now, and to hell with the future.

All of these attitudes will prevent you from being in the flow, because when we are estranged from our physical selves we cannot enjoy our bodily existence, and we certainly can't be grateful for it. If we are out of contact with the natural rhythms of our bodies, how can we be fully sensitive to the rhythms of the universe that make up synchronicity? So, take a moment, and review the messages you send yourself each day.

Decoding the Messages of Love and Sex

One of the biggest stumbling blocks to flow, to being at peace with the way the future unfolds, is the most unexpected: love. One would think love would help us to be accepting of others and to let go of trying to control. While it's true that the highest form of love will do that, unfortunately there are quite a few other forms of passionate attachment that will not let this happen. Of these, sexual love is often the most difficult.

In the modern world, sexual love is so tied up with questions of hope, fear, doubt, and power inequalities that the whole experience of enjoying our sexuality may feel like picking our way through a minefield. When we are in love, we may be worried that we love more deeply than our partner, leading us to feel anxious and vulnerable in case our partner deserts us for another. This hurts, of course; moreover, if we do actually love the other person more than we are loved in return, it may also make us look bad in the eyes of those we know, so the danger exists for double hurt. The hurt deepens still further if we separate or divorce and have to divide up our belongings.

The popular press isn't much help, either. Pass through any supermarket checkout display and it is guaranteed you'll find brightly colored magazines like *Cosmopolitan* or *Men's Health* full of articles offering detailed directions on advanced sexual techniques to make him/her go wild. The explicit message is that with this knowledge you can establish yourself as the more powerful partner in your relationship, with a lover who won't leave because the sex will never be as good with anyone else—unless, of course, that other person has also read the magazine. The implicit message is that you are not adequate as you are.

Alongside these magazines are other magazines dedicated to the breakups and affairs of Hollywood stars and other glitterati. Sometimes I wonder if those famous people shouldn't perhaps just check out those advanced sexual techniques in the lifestyle magazines, so they wouldn't have these troubles—but perhaps I'm missing something here.

What this booby trap by the cash register leads us to believe is this: it's not safe to be in love with anyone, even if you're a movie star. Everyone cheats and lies and winds up miserable. And this happens even if we've done our homework reading up on the "Ten Ways to Touch Your Guy/Gal." Fear has thus been firmly inserted into the realm of sex and intimacy.

The anxiety is everywhere. These days, even if you're a man who finds himself in love, the TV is only too happy to tell you that you are at risk of having erectile dysfunction. But don't worry. Just check out this advertisement for Viagra™ or Cialis™ and ask your doctor for prescription drugs and you'll be just fine. These endless ads definitely raise anxiety in the male population. In a self-fulfilling prophecy, a man may genuinely start to fear that he's not fully potent. And at the same time, his partner may feel that he/she is to blame in some way for not being attractive enough, understanding enough, charming enough. So, better get those pills now, just in case... I think you can see how this works. Fear grows.

The realm of loving sex, trust, and warmth in a relationship (which may or may not include wild passionate couplings with every imaginable variation and using pleasure-enhancing devices) is under siege in our modern era. Today, many people waste a lot of precious energy feeling jealous, deceived, possessive, controlling, angry, and inadequate, and continue to feel that way for a large part of their adult lives. With so many troubling issues to consider in the realm of relationships, it's hard for many people to relax, feel the love, and enter the flow of the relationship. Many of us are left wondering whether our relationship is as good as it could be, as good as someone else's (as if we'd actually know), or whether we're communicating effectively with each other.

In an age where there is more sex available more easily than ever before, where birth control eases the edge of the most obvious consequence of sex, we still have a massive sex industry. Prostitution is a boom profession. And it is so, in part, because it offers sex divorced from most of the issues we've just listed. It's sex that is anonymous and faceless, so no one can comment on how well or badly we do it, or what we do, or how we go about asking for what we want. For the right payment, the prostitute can become whatever it is the person paying wants for that short period of time. The only reproach later will be if one gets caught.

I think you can see that there might be some appeal in all this for the person who pays for sex—and there may, of course, be many other reasons blended in there. I think you will also feel deep sadness for a society that has made this so prevalent as an imagined solution for what ails it. In every instance this is simply about the ego trying to console itself.

The point here is not to give up on love. Real love is worth everything. We have to see, rather, that as a society we have built into our experience of love a large number of difficulties that don't have to be there if we shift our consciousness. We have to choose what we want to accept into our lives and firmly reject the rest.

Decoding the Messages in the Work Place

"Work has a habit of getting in the way of everything." Or at least that's what one of my co-workers said to me the other day, and we had a good laugh about it. Behind the joke lay the somewhat more serious consideration that for many people what they do for most of their productive waking life feels neither engaging nor vital, it's a bore that happens to provide money and is often an excellent source of complaints, anxiety, and swirling emotions. That's where we lose sight of the flow.

When I first began teaching at the college level, I noticed a marked tendency among my fellow teachers to share horror stories about their students. Some of these tales were instructive, but most were merely the start of a spiral that led the speakers and listeners into a negative space of despair. When I was asked to run the department, we instituted meetings in which I proposed that there would be no "war stories" like this; instead, we'd focus on what worked for our students.

When I first floated this idea, the room fell silent. "So what are we supposed to talk about?" asked one person. Literally, these people did not know what to say to each other if they weren't complaining. It wasn't that they weren't good teachers, but rather that they'd become so used to filling their minds with how bad things were that they couldn't let go of this mind-set, even though they hated it.

Over the next several months, we gradually changed the atmosphere by focusing on and sharing strategies that worked, and as we did so the individuals concerned began to think more creatively, form working friendships, and see more possibilities. Some still held out for their own dark ways of thinking, but they gradually stopped trying to derail things; some just stopped coming to the meetings altogether, which was a relief.

The point here is not that a miraculous change had happened, because it hadn't. What had occurred was that a whole roomful of people had seen the mental habits they'd adopted about their work and decided to change them. Work became less of a chore and more of a pleasure. Individual teachers clung less tightly to their syllabus (the ego telling them that this was the one and only way to get things done), and they began to work more with their students.

Personally, I'm always in favor of working with people rather than working in service to what is outlined on pieces of paper. When we did this at my college—when we responded to what was in the classroom rather than what we thought ought to be in the room—then we all gave ourselves the chance to experience the flow. It's an example of how work can shift from Hell to Heaven depending on how you approach it. So, how do you approach *your* work? Does it feel like an authentic experience to you? If not, how could you make your work feel more vital for you?

One way to try and break through your habitual feelings about work and find out what you are truly feeling is to monitor yourself closely and listen to your body. Do you get a stomach ache or feel butterflies around certain people? Do you find yourself sweating when you have to deal with certain tasks that are mentally demanding, as opposed to physically demanding? How much do you need to "bite your tongue" at work? Do you feel the urge to write sarcastic e-mails in response to e-mails you feel to be aggressive or annoying? Do you feel under attack? Do certain people make you feel gloomy?

It's likely you've had all of these feelings at work at some point. These are symptoms, but it's up to you to decide what these experiences are trying to tell you. How much of your soul are you willing to give away in order to get that paycheck?

Being in the flow doesn't mean that you banish feelings of discomfort; instead, you shift your relationship to what is happening. You are able to shrug off small annoyances because you know you're engaged in something more vital. In fact, you will start to feel more energized by your work, once you agree to disregard the obstacles.

But before you can make that change, you'll have to start doing a few things differently. Try this. When you leave work for the day, take a hint from the birds. Have you ever watched birds, like pigeons or ducks, when they squabble? They get all fluffed up and noisy, then they part, and each bird does a sort of fluttering shrug, resettles his or her feathers, then carries on. I call it throwing off the negative energy, and recent research has shown that they are, in fact, working off excess adrenaline in this fashion. This is instinctual for many birds and mammals but not, alas, for humans. We tend to hold on to our negative emotions. I learned about this first from some t'ai chi teachers, who literally would cup their hands and sweep the negative energy from their bodies after a hard day, shaking it off their fingertips like water. [1]

The lesson was clear: there is a lot of negative energy around, and it has to be swept aside. By doing this movement, you are telling your unconscious that this is only negative energy, it can be cleared, and you're not about to take it home with you. Your unconscious will cooperate with you and let go of your stress. It sounds simple; it is simple. And it works. I like to do the shrug as often as I can because tension builds in my shoulders, and it feels good to give them a bit of a twitch anyway.

Another technique is hand washing. After a tough day I'll go and wash my hands, and sometimes my face, before I leave. It's important to do this mindfully, otherwise one can wind up staring into the mirror, looking at the extra lines and gray hair, and feeling ground down. If you allow this to get out of hand, you may become gloomy and feel that you have to hide in the washroom, and that's not a good message to send yourself. Instead, think of it as before, as a way of clearing your energy, because you don't want to take this stuff home with you. Approached in this way you can find real benefits to these simple actions, and even more so if you tell yourself why you are doing this. It's a form of ritual that reminds us how we wish to live.

My own ritual of leaving work includes such things as making sure I hold doors for others as I leave the building, rather than rushing through, and if I drive I make sure to let other cars go first. Most people are anxious to get home, so it's actually a good idea to be out of the way of anxious drivers. I do it for another reason, though. I do it to remind myself that I'm going home, where I want the atmosphere to be helpful and considerate, and I may as well practice that along the way. I've tried jumping in my car and racing back home in order to complain about my colleagues. I did it for years. It wastes a perfectly good evening.

And that brings us neatly to the concept of how you can deal with this if you're working from home. Be very careful about this, or you will turn your entire home into your workplace, and you'll never actually leave work.

In my home, I make sure there's a specific place for my "work" activities. I have a desk, but if I decide that I want to work at the dining room table for a change, I clear just a section to use, not the whole table. This sends me a couple of messages at a subliminal level. The first is, this is a dining room, and office work is only happening here as a temporary thing. Life, real life, will come along and force me to stop—usually at the weekends when people come to dine. This forces me to tidy up and file things. Otherwise, they'd get out of hand entirely.

I also make sure not to take my paperwork over to the couch, or into the bedroom, because that is what I call work-creep. If you are lucky enough to have a home office, then that is where the work stays. Remember, you work for the money. If you didn't get paid you probably wouldn't do it. You need to be able to walk away from it at the end of the day and get another perspective. You owe it to the work to do this, because without this separation your quality of work will suffer drastically. You want to do your best? Then do a little less.

When I was a student, I shared a place with a person who allowed work-creep into his life all the time. At one point, he had the engine of the motorcycle he was working on placed firmly on the kitchen table, propped up with books about literary theory (his other area of expertise), and pieces of carburetor were spread around the bathroom. We never seemed to be able to escape the smell and presence of grease and motor oil. Clearly, certain types of work belong in specific places.

With respect to my own work—writing, which is something I love to do—the same understandings apply. I write happily, willingly, and probably never actually stop writing in my head, as new ideas are constantly popping up (which is why I have a notebook to hand whenever possible). But much as I love it, I know that writing for

16 hours straight, then falling into bed to do it again the next day, is not a good idea. The writing becomes very bad.

So here is what I do. First thing in the morning, I'm able to contact my inner flow more easily than at most other times because the unconscious has been bubbling away all night. As a result, when I sit at the keyboard I'm ready to write things that I didn't know I had inside me. The flow can begin. I usually get a couple of hours of writing in before I need to start teaching.

I also know another thing about flow, and that is we have to respect it. If you take the time to love the experience, you can treat it like a box of delicious candies. You take one or two now and really enjoy them, knowing that you can do the same tomorrow. If you try to eat them all now, then you'll just feel sick and, worse, have a sugar high. I call this approach "loving your writing," because you want to enjoy it, not to get it done and finished as soon as possible. When we do this something miraculous happens—the chocolate box is never empty.

On the other hand, when we try to force things along, wolfing down the chocolates, we tell our subconscious that we don't believe the good things will be there tomorrow, that this is a once-in-a-lifetime opportunity. If that's the message you are acting out, then guess what happens? Your unconscious agrees with you and shuts off the flow. The next day there's nothing happening. The inspiration has dried up. You're written out. You've misused the flow.

My example is taken from writing, because that's what I know best and I have worked with enough writers to know that it's exactly like this for many of them, too. It's my contention that this same circumstance is true for almost all creative work. Allow creativity space in your life. Give it attention for the amount of time that feels right and manageable to you. Then, make sure you get the other stuff in your life working, too. Don't force things. Take a walk around a park, be outside, run an errand, but only after you've done your creative work. The aim is to bring the work you love into your life, suffusing your day with what you love to do. Do not stop living so that you become only the work.

The way many people think of this creative activity is that it's very like meditation or prayer. You allow a certain amount of time for it each day or week and you respect that time. Now, you may not like the religious context of the word prayer, but I'd defend it by pointing out that in the early medieval period of European history there were so many "holy-days" (holidays) and festivals, that approximately one day in every four was a day off. At such times, people would have various rituals and rites, and these would include songs, the acting of Biblical or mythic themes, races and contests, pilgrimages both long and short, and considerable amounts of time spent decorating the shrines and temples with flowers, pictures, and various offerings. In fact, expressive creativity was practically mandated in the religious calendar—and in the final analysis, all of it came under the heading of "prayer."

Those religious leaders might have known a thing or two they can relay to us. The first is that we have to make room for creativity; we have to value it—not as a sideline but as a mainline in our lives. The second is that work has rhythms. Today, we live by the factory whistle and the 7 a.m. power breakfast meeting, and we don't even try to get into an easeful rhythm of work: the average assembly line is calculated on efficiency and profit, not on what makes the work force feel good; instead of real job satisfaction, we have wage increases.

This method of incentivizing workers has been known for at least 200 years. When the world's first factories were set up in England's mill districts in about 1750, the owners were puzzled about productivity. The workers would sit at the looms and, as they had done in their villages for generations, they would sing along together and work their looms in time to the tunes. But this rhythm wasn't fast enough for the factory bosses, who wanted more profits, so they banned singing. The songs were lost, the rhythms of work were lost, and workers died young, exhausted, and penniless. But the mills made a profit.

The rhythms that could sustain work had evolved over hundreds of years, but they were swept away in less than a decade. Do we know what we've lost in pursuit of efficiency?

So ask yourself: Do you try to "push things through" at work? Is the goal more valued than the process? And who says that? Is the company's profit more important than the people in the company? What's the company for, in that case? Let your work become a prayer, and a connection to what is holy.

If we are mindful of these things, we can identify the barriers to being in the flow. Then we can strategize ways to make sure that we can live in this world, where so much is out of balance, and still maintain a strong sense of what is important to us, of what will fulfill us and keep us in touch with our creativity, every day.

A person who is out of contact with real creativity does not lose that ability. Instead, the energy has to go somewhere, and it can only go in a couple of directions. The first place thwarted creativity can go is inward, into depression. As I mentioned earlier, depression afflicts one in 10 Americans today—that's the number who are taking antidepressants at any one time. There are also thousands of people who are depressed but can't afford the medication, or who resort to alcohol and illegal substances. Depression and self-destruction go hand in hand.

The second direction for thwarted creativity is outwards, into anger—usually manifested in crime and antisocial behaviors of many sorts. In the United States, we incarcerate our citizens at the highest rate in the world. The very poor and the underprivileged are disproportionately over-represented in our prison systems, which are overcrowded and going broke. So we're really good at driving people mad and locking them up in this society. And in case we forget, there's no shortage of people who use their considerable creativity to create tax loopholes and pursue the sorts of investment strategies that are "legal" but not moral. We have only to think of the hedge fund and derivatives scandals and the collapses that have dogged Wall Street, and so on. It's creativity in motion, but it has no real benefit for the greater society. Just ask someone who has had his home foreclosed upon recently.

What This Can Tell Us

So let me spell this out. Being in the flow is about aligning ourselves with the energy of the Universe, or God energy, or the Creator, or whatever we wish to call it, and it has as many forms as we can imagine. Here I have equated it with creativity, for it is when we follow our creative urges that unusual and unexpected things happen and new creations occur. Creativity seen in the widest sense is not just about art; it's about everything we do. Art, though, serves as a handy metaphor. Real creativity does not seek to recreate slavish copies of what has already been produced—it makes things new. It responds to inspiration.

The exercise of creativity leads us, inevitably, to synchronous events that reassure and support the person doing the creating, since at that point it is less about the ego rewards and more about being a servant of the creative urge. The ancients knew this when they saw the artist as needing to follow a discipline, much of it very strict, in order to serve the art and craft of the creative endeavor properly. This was not about a trendy artist from a New York gallery making several million dollars overnight. At its highest levels, this was the team of artisans and craftsmen who came together to create the great cathedrals of Europe, the great temples of Japan, and the magnificent courts of the Forbidden City.

The discipline involved in working as part of an artistic team actually freed the artists from all the traps I've just listed—disruptions caused by unbalanced situations in love, work, use of language, thinking, and frailties of the body - simply because the work always came first. Any of these traps can destroy the access we might have to being in the flow and being able to experience the synchronicity that awaits us. Any of them can lead us away from the primacy of the heart and back to the ego-space.

The very best way to circumvent any barriers that may arise is to do the personal internal work of the descent into the self, for after we have looked inside ourselves in the specific ways we've discussed, we'll have attained the necessary centeredness to allow these other issues not to overwhelm us. We have to remind ourselves of that. This struggle exists everyday. Here is what Charles Swindoll has to say about it:

> The remarkable thing is we have a choice everyday regarding the attitude we will embrace from that day. We cannot change our past, we cannot change the fact that people will act in certain way. We cannot change the inevitable. The only thing that we can do is play on the one string that we have and this string is, attitude. I am convinced that life is 10 percent what happens to me and 90 percent how I react to it. And so it is with you... We are in charge of our attitudes. [2]

The final quality we need is the courage to commit to what we choose to do. Here is W. H. Murray, describing the changes he felt when, after some hesitation, he declared he would go on a Himalayan expedition:

> But when I said that nothing had been done I erred in one important matter. We had definitely committed ourselves and were halfway out of our ruts. We had put down our passage money—booked a sailing to Bombay. This may sound too simple, but is great in consequence. Until one is committed, there is hesitancy, the chance to draw back, always ineffectiveness. Concerning all acts of initiative (and creation), there is one elementary truth the ignorance of which kills countless ideas and splendid plans: that the moment one definitely commits oneself, then providence moves too.
>
> A whole stream of events issues from the decision, raising in one's favor all manner of unforeseen incidents, meetings and material assistance, which no man could have dreamt would have come his way. I learned a deep respect for one of Goethe's couplets: "Whatever you can do or dream you can, begin it. Boldness has genius, power and magic in it!" [3]

Committing ourselves to a course of action that is authentic will bring us into the flow of synchronicity, and just as W.H. Murray says, it will also take us out of our comfort zone of familiar surroundings. It is not possible for us to enter the flow and expect to have the tidy lives we already have. Synchronicity does not exist to make our ordinary lives easier. It exists so that we can take on larger, more important struggles, and do whatever it is the Universe needs us to do. When we boldly free ourselves from restricting thoughts and take on our life's work, whether it is climbing a mountain or becoming an artist, we move into harmony with synchronicity. We cannot then slink back to an anonymous existence in which we think small, and live safe lives, without falling out of the flow of synchronicity.

Friends

Choose Them Wisely

If we are to be fully aware of the stumbling blocks we'll face, then we'll have to take a close look at just a few more since some of them may be unexpected—and that includes who we have as friends.

You can't choose your family, but you can choose your friends. So goes the saying. Ask yourself if that is true for you. Did you choose your friends, or did you allow them to choose you? It may be that in selecting you they gave you a great gift, and that you can learn from them as you enjoy being with them. It may also be that some of them chose you because you allow them to reinforce some rather negative habits that they hold dear, and some of that thinking is rubbing off on you.

We need to be as careful of whom we have as friends as of what we eat, because we all have come across toxic people, and many of them will want to make you their friend. And the same thing goes for you—you may wish to bring people into your life because they agree with you, and perhaps some of the thoughts that you want them to agree with are not that charitable, compassionate, or elevated.

Most of us can be friendly to almost anyone. That's just what living in a society is all about. We have to learn to get along. Yet we also need to be sure that we are allowing those people who are good-willed and helpful into our lives. Nothing will waste your time more completely, nor keep you from the accepting path of love and compassion more effectively, than a high-maintenance or selfish friend.

If you are to value the experience of flow, and stay within it, then you may need to observe closely how your friends run their lives. Do they seek to dump their problems on you? Are they gossips, spreading half-understood stories or alarmist "facts" about your shared experiences? Do they seek to dominate you by giving advice that you don't want or organizing your life in ways that you don't challenge? The point here is to see if you can spend more time with people who bring you real delight, who help you see the world as a finer, more joyous place.

It's hard to make this sort of call, because some people seem to defy easy identification. Many years ago I had a colleague who wished to be my friend; she was a worthy, moral person. Yet her way of dealing with the world was to identify a project in which she could become a sort of "savior." So she would take up a cause, like the fate of seal pups in the Arctic, and insist that everyone she knew adopt this crusade. When that was over, it might be the earthquake victims in China or the orphans of Sarajevo. This was all thoroughly worthy work, and I'm sure she achieved many truly wonderful things. The question to ask is not whether the projects were right for her (clearly they were) but whether they were right for the other people involved.

If you have such a person in your life, ask if these crusades are authentic to who you are and how you prefer to operate. I did not choose to join this woman, my friend, in her activities because, for me, she was approaching the tasks in a spirit of anger—anger that not enough was being done for the situation as she saw it. I'm not sure more anger was what was needed, so I gave what I could in terms of time and money and decided, as Thich Nhat Hanh says, that "peace is every step": if I could not bring help and peace, then this specific way of proceeding was not for me.[1] The drama and swirl created by my erstwhile friend was not, in fact, helping very much, and her tendency to throw herself into a task that would burn her out was not helpful in the long term to anyone, I felt.

You may have to review your friends carefully. Do you feel peaceful when you are with them? Do you leave conversations with them feeling as if you've been energized, that you've learned something or seen with new eyes? If so, then you have a friendship that may well be highly productive. Do you feel you are an equal contributor, or more of a receiver? Real friendships are built, and built strongly, because each person can give to the other. If you feel yourself to be more of a giver or more of a receiver you may well have an admirable rapport, but it may be unbalanced. In such cases there may be enormous and powerful loyalty, yet no real equality. Value the loyalty, and don't stop searching for the equal friendship that will power your life forward.

For most people, friendship is a fairly shallow concept, reduced to the level of buddy-ship. Following the same teams, engaging in the same leisure activities, whether they be flying kites or playing golf: these are the things many people regard as friendships. I'd put it in more specific terms. A real friend sees who you are and loves you even with all your faults. That is why a friend will challenge you when you are making a foolish move or will disagree with you—because a friendship that depends upon one person repressing or denying something that is true is not a true friendship.

One woman I worked with told me a heart-rending tale about her disagreement with a friend. This woman decided that she'd risk losing the friendship forever rather than not speak up. As she said: "I couldn't live with myself if I didn't say something; and I knew I'd rather sacrifice the friendship than agree with what was wrong. I won't agree to a lie for the sake of a friendship." These are powerful words. How many of us would have the courage to speak out? How many of us would refuse to put up with a friendship where there were certain disagreements that couldn't ever be mentioned if that friendship were to continue? How many of us would have come to a polite compromise?

If we take this one step farther, I'd argue that loving a friend in this fashion is a way of experiencing unconditional love. The woman who was protesting was not ceasing to love her friend. She was, instead, asking her friend to live up to some high expectations, and was therefore loving her more, not less.

In this world, it's true that you get what you decide to put up with. If you accept second best, then that's about what you'll get. And if you have second-best people in your life, their presence will stop you from being able to connect with the best people who are out there and the best part of yourself. You simply won't see what else is available, or if you do see it, you won't have time to welcome it into your life because you already have all this second-rate stuff going on.

Worse still, second-rate people will try to pull you down to their level, every time. They feel more comfortable when you're not doing well, when you're not happy. In fact, your successes will be troubling to them because success makes them ask why they haven't managed more success in their own lives. And that might take some difficult decisions for them. It might mean rearranging all sorts of cozy agreements, and that means work. It might demand honesty and integrity and action. No wonder they'd prefer to pull you down.

> **EXERCISE:** Make a list of friends in a column on a piece of paper wide enough for five columns. In the second column, list a couple of things beside each friend that you can't change: one attribute that you admire, and one that you don't like. Your list might look like this:

Millie: *Would give you anything you ask for*   *Obsessively talks about her kids*

When you've done this for several people you may want to select from the list a couple of friends to focus on, and ask yourself: what it would take to change those behaviors? This is what you write in the third column:

Millie might stop talking obsessively about her kids if... they were all successfully grown up and settled in life, perhaps?

Now, for column number four, imagine that the event in column number three has happened:

Millie's kids are all grown up and gone. Wouldn't she just start talking about her grandchildren instead? And as for her generosity, she'd stop doing that only when she felt she didn't have to offer things and could offer something else.
What would that be? Write it down.

Now, make your fifth and last column. Write about the following: What are the advantages for you in keeping everything just the way it is?

Usually, what we discover when I do this exercise with people in my groups is that the very things they complain about in their friends, such as the compulsive talking or the sometimes oppressive generosity, are exactly the things that they don't want to change *because if they changed them they would have to become more real with these people*, and that would take work. It might not even be fun. If Millie didn't talk about her kids all the time, then she might reveal herself as needy, sad, and unhappy in her marriage, and perhaps we wouldn't want to have to deal with that. Her generosity might hide a fundamental lack of real self-esteem and be a disguise for emotional neediness. As things stand now, we can feel affection for Millie, recognize that she's useful, and keep her at a distance. That's convenient. It's neighborly, too, because we don't have to get closer than we may wish. But let's not pretend it's real friendship.

Take the time right now to do this exercise and consider your friends in new ways. It may take some time to feel your way through this, so don't rush. You may even have to hold this idea for a few days before you see your way forward.

Every choice we make, every behavior, holds a perceived advantage. That's why we persist in sticking with them. Sometimes, though, the advantage is not what we actually need.

We can take this farther. Friendships are often microcosms of the way we run our worlds, which is why this topic is so essential. Do we indulge vague complaints about our "friends" and in the process allow ourselves a sneaking sense of superiority, rather than attempting real intimacy? We can choose to fill up our minds and our hearts with anything we wish, but are we choosing the best things we are capable of? The problem may not be Millie; it might be us.

This five-column exercise, if done with care, will show us several things. It will show us those people we put up with and call our friends, and why we do it. Yet it can also tell us who actually is a friend. We will find that we can see the faults in others, the things that puzzle us, and that we accept them, because we recognize the real loving nature that lies behind the behavior. As one man put it, describing a friend of many years, "He annoys the heck out of me, and I can't help loving him anyway."

Summary

In this second part of the book, I've given you a variety of situations to consider. If you wish to keep them unchallenged, it is easy to defend them with good logical reasoning; yet, all of them will keep any one of us from being fully in the flow of life. My task here has been to take what might be unconscious for many of us and make it fully conscious. Only then can we deal with these issues.

If we are to accept flow into our lives, and pave the way for synchronicity, we will need to pay attention to these issues. First of all, we must listen to the language we use to describe our lives and decide whether it is appropriate or accurate. Language creates concepts and shapes beliefs, so we must be selective and critical or we may convince ourselves of what is not true. These are the building blocks for the thoughts we hold, and many of them may turn out to be simply prejudices that we have sought to confirm by selecting the evidence that supports our biases. We must examine these beliefs as if they belonged to someone else, or we will be entrapped by them.

Similarly, as we've seen, we could do worse than to listen to the messages our body sends us, as opposed to attempting to shut down those communications. This powerful preverbal current of energy will set us on the right path every time—but only if we listen to its nonverbal language and know what it's saying.

Bodily urges, however, can be unruly, so we must also take care that the world of physical love and sex, with its powerful ability to override other feelings, does not so fill our lives that we cannot see what else is happening.

This overlaps fully with the world of work and how we choose to lead our work lives and careers. What we decide to believe about work is essentially what we believe about our whole world—until we hit a rock, perhaps in midlife, and we feel that all our beliefs about what we do may need to be rethought. Such occasions can be shattering.

And just as we have work colleagues we like and value, we also have friends who share our lives. The wrong friends can be as limiting as the wrong career. Our tendency to hide this from our highest consciousness is an even greater danger, since friends and family are, for many of us, the reason we do what we do. If they let us down we may find we have nothing to lean on at all. That, at least, is the fear.

Once again I'd like to repeat what I said earlier. These sections on the traps we can fall into are not here in order to criticize or condemn anyone. My hope is that these words will function as warnings, and that, also, they will allow us to see situations with real understanding. Many of our friends are not consciously trying to get in our way; yet, they still might do that if they are not fully conscious and if we're not alert.

When we do see what's going on, we can grow in understanding and move toward compassion, since I'm sure we have also done the same things ourselves. Like Dante walking through Hell, we have no need to condemn those who are already suffering, locked in their chosen ways of not getting free. They deserve our compassion for they are just like us. And, exactly like Dante, we must learn from what we notice, so we don't make the same mistakes. The traps of the ego are everywhere.

CHAPTER 17

Further Barriers to Synchronicity

Family

Family issues can be all consuming. Even in the most loving situation, family members and family politics can cause us to be reactive and so prevent us from being alert to what is going on now—unaware of even the existence of flow, let alone learning to use it to improve our life experience. Obviously, many families are supportive, but there's always some dispute somewhere, something that will keep us off balance.

The reason for this is straightforward: our families have developed a history with us that began long before we were born, and because of who they are, their words count more than other people's. We can ignore what they say, but it takes far more energy to "forget" an unkind word from a family member than it does to discard the same comment coming from somewhere else. In fact, we may never forget something that was said carelessly—even though we pretend we have erased it.

Even harder to assess are family understandings and habits of thought, many of which are never spelled out in any coherent form. Children as young as four and five are already beginning to play games and think about what their own family will look like when they grow up to be parents themselves. We can be pretty sure that those receptive young minds are already putting together a vision of how they want the future to be long before they even know the facts of life. Many of those projections are carried forward pretty much unchanged into adulthood. Such unspoken attitudes have occasionally been handed on from generation to generation. No wonder they're so hard to alter.

This is not always a problem. It's part of the family or social group's folkways, or culture. But it can have a negative aspect. An unloving or self-involved parent can do a huge amount of damage by clinging to this unconscious projection when real life may turn out to be very different.

Here in the West, where the nuclear family or some version of it is the model we see most frequently, the small size of the family system makes things more difficult. Removed from a traditional village environment full of relatives and lifelong residents, as found in some other societies, we find ourselves in a familial setup which, for the most part, is restricted to just the immediate family members, living close to other suburban homes in which strangers or mere acquaintances reside. The family becomes claustrophobic under such circumstances, so parental approval or disapproval has more emotional weight.

Here's an example. Just the other day, a school in a town here in Massachusetts barred parents from attending the district's basketball finals because parents, it seemed, tended to argue with the referees, shout unpleasant things from the sidelines, and fight with other parents. One could blame a few troublemakers, or one could observe that the investment of some parents in their children being on the winning team was, somehow, out of balance with reality. This is surely a result of that over-involved and claustrophobic family system I've been describing.

There was also the incident of the 250-pound male parent who disagreed with something the 120-pound female superintendent of schools said in a private conference, so he punched her in the face and broke her nose. Notice: this is the parent we're talking about. I could add further examples, but they would merely be sad instances of parental confusions.

For our purposes, the important point is to recall that family over-involvement has a tendency to create discord. And discord will keep anyone out of the flow, any time. So a quick rule of thumb is this: anything a parent or family member says has approximately five times more power to upset or console you than the same words said by anyone else. This means that such people have five times, at least, as much capability to shred your sense of calm.

Since we form our sense of personal ego (what we like, who we care for, and why) in large measure in those early years when we are at home living in a family, I think you can see how powerful this is. We respond to our parents' praise or displeasure out of our ego-space, because when we're young that's pretty much all we've got. And as we know, when we operate out of our ego-space, we're not operating out of our heart-space. We take offense more quickly, and we require praise more urgently, from our family.

Here's an example that may help. One man reported how at his ninth birthday party his mother seemed disapproving. Afterward, she said to him that his friends were not up to the standard she'd expected. The boy was puzzled at the time, for these were his school friends, the kids from neighboring families who often car-pooled. Who was he supposed to have for friends? The puzzlement was genuine, and the blow to his ego larger than he realized.

He noticed, decades later, that from that day forward, he brought very few of his friends home, and he kept that habit in place into his thirties. It was too insulting, he felt, to have to lay himself open in that way. Now, perhaps the mother was socially ambitious, or perhaps she simply wanted the best for her son. We can't know. We can only observe that the damage was done, see how it happened, and try to be alert for the future. Ego hurts ego, but it cannot hurt the person who insists on working from the heart.

We all are likely to respond to perceived slights this way, by receiving them when we are in an ego-space. That's simply an old habit. We were trying to develop our healthy egos as kids, and so, when we're around parents or family we tend to slip back into old habits of thinking, ego habits of being. It's a trap, and we need to be aware of it to avoid it.

Smile, shrug it off, and send the person love anyway.

Here's another comparison that may help. Imagine the family all sitting together in a car. You're all there, strapped in with seatbelts and the doors locked, and you're all going whichever way the decision-makers in the family think you ought to be going, never mind whether you fully agree with that destination. It's the family vacation trip, and the car is full of stuff. Now imagine that the car gets a flat tire, and you're miles from anywhere. Perhaps there isn't even cell phone connectivity. The driver doesn't want to stop and fix the flat, but elects to drive on, ever more slowly, as the tire shreds itself. Everyone's hoping a garage will appear. You can imagine the scenario.

This is what tends to happen when a family hits some sort of crisis that they don't know how to deal with. They decide to keep everything and everyone in place, and just try and tough it out. Why? Because jacking the car up and changing the wheel would mean getting everyone out of the car, making sure no one wanders off, taking out all the stuff in the trunk, finding the toolkit, and so on. It would mean a major reorganization of everything, especially the baggage. And if it's raining, you have even less desire to do that.

Now, if you were on your own in your own car, you wouldn't do that, I suspect. You'd get out and either try to fix the flat or flag down another motorist. Either way, because you're on your own it's easier to put things right. The family, because it is a unit locked into certain patterns and ways of doing things, isn't quite as good at taking the radical steps required.

If you feel this scenario is true for your family, then it may well be time to strike out on your own. The cohesion that makes families strong can often prevent them from changing with the altering circumstances of real life. Support them, love them, be loyal to them, but be loyal to yourself first.

Tests, and Why we Need Them

All of the items I've mentioned since Chapter 10 have been the sorts of things that can test us. Perhaps the single most important thing—and the most difficult, too—is to remember that we will all be tested. The guiding hand of fate, of God, of the Divinity, will give us many good things. It will also give us some hard passages to cope with. This seems unfair. After all, if we're doing the best we can to understand what's happening, why should we be treated harshly?

It's a good question. Our best response is to realize that in order to do what it has to do the Universe needs us to be as strong as possible, so it tests us to see how well we've internalized the lessons. Because we're human, we have a wonderful ability to take in information that we can forget in a few seconds when we're under stress. The important thing is to try to remember to be loving even in the face of tremendous provocation and distress, to remain optimistic even when all seems to be falling apart. When we do this, we grow our inner strength and develop our inner faith. We have to be able to talk the good words and do the good works, as well.

This is important, because there are three ways of knowing something. The first is to know that something exists. For example, I know Mongolia exists, but I don't spend much time thinking about it. The second sort of knowledge is to know about something in an abstract way: I can read about Mongolia and find out lots of things about its composition and weather. The third way of knowing is experiential: I can go and live in Mongolia. The tests we're talking about demand we know our lives at all three levels.

Tests are always about the ego. "Why should fate do this to me?" is a question that has to do with ME, and what I feel I deserve, or the way I feel things ought to be. Yet, as we know, it's not about me; it's about giving over control to a greater power than ourselves and having faith in it. The world needs people who are going to do some heavy lifting and help move us all into a place of greater love and compassion. It doesn't need us to whine or complain. Christian Larson writes about this powerfully:

> Resolve to remain as strong, as determined, and as highly
> enthused during the darkest night of adversity as you are during
> the sunniest day of prosperity. Do not feel disappointed when

things seem disappointing. [...] The man who never weakens when things are against him will grow stronger and stronger until all things delight to be for him. He will finally have all the strength he may desire or need. Be always strong and you will always be stronger. [1]

He is echoed by the mystic Eileen Caddy, who writes:

Let your faith be strong and unshakeable. Be glad and rejoice when your faith is put to the test, for this strengthens it until it becomes as a rock, able to withstand the storms and tempests of life without being shaken in any way. [2]

These sentiments have echoed through the ages, in one form or another, and whether we as readers believe the exact doctrine of the original writers or not is hardly the point. Each writer was describing an essential psychological process that is, in essence, always the same. Following the path the guiding hand wishes to lead us down requires us to have courage, and above all to grow that courage and faith. Tests will allow courage to grow. Only then can we play our part fully in the great, incomprehensible pattern that we are called to join.

Imagine you start to write the novel or poem or memoir you've always felt you needed to. You feel the inspiration; you start to write. Later that night someone calls, perhaps a former friend who has been cruel to you, and the temptation is to be upset, angry, sad—and give up the task you had started with such energy mere hours before. That's a test. Are you going to continue with what you know needs to be done, or are you going to slip into self-pity?

I use this example because it has happened to me, and similar things have happened to other people I've talked to. It's been surprisingly common as a test. The lesson for me was hard but simple. Let the other person's attitude go and *hold no resentment*. When we forgive, we let go of such feelings. For if I cannot write with forgiveness in my heart, then what sort of writing will I be producing?

CHAPTER 18

Still More Barriers

Illness

Illness can also be a test—perhaps the hardest. It will take up a huge amount of time and energy and anxiety, and in many ways it's one of the most difficult things for any of us to face, since it seems to come from outside, dropped upon us by the unkind hand of fate.

Yet, I'm also aware from my own experience that illness can come about because of things we are doing to ourselves, the ways we run our lives, the ways we eat or live. Illness can be a wakeup blaring of trumpets, if we're ready to think differently. It can be a spiritual path, too, since we are required to remain ourselves and not become merely passive amid the seemingly random orders of doctors and physicians of all kinds. Here are the words of Dr. Christiane Northrup, author of *Women's Bodies, Women's Wisdom*:

> My task is not to kill the messenger of my illness by ignoring it,
> complaining about it, or simply suppressing my symptoms.
> My task is to examine my life with compassion and honesty and
> identify the places that are crying out for love, acceptance,
> harmony, and fulfillment. [1]

This is a very illuminating way of seeing things, and surely it must be a part, at least, of the process of healing.

Yet, so often, people attach to their identity as a sufferer from a particular ailment, and they identify with the disease to such an extent that they cannot let it go without diminishing their sense of who they are. This is simply another ego-trap. If we say we are someone who suffers from x or y, we have a recognizable identity for others to latch on to, and we have reasons for living the way we do.

It can also work the other way. When we don't want to do something we can claim physical frailties if we wish to. I can't visit Aunt Maud because I'm allergic to her cats; I can't go skiing because of my knee, wrist, ankles, and so on. A dear friend of mine who is a vegetarian wanted very much to travel in the deserts of North Africa, where almost every type of restaurant food contained some sort of meat. It was easiest, she discovered, to say there was a medical reason for her dietary choice, as she couldn't make people understand that she didn't want to eat animals. Health excuses are very useful in getting what we want.

This leads us to ask to what extent are illnesses reflections of psychic imbalances, and to what extent are they things we hide behind? Louise Hay has some extensive and very useful charts in her excellent book *You Can Heal Your Life* in which she links illnesses to psychological areas of unreconciled pain or tension. [2] This is a familiar idea from traditional Chinese and Ayurvedic medicine, with considerable empirical backing.

For example, those who suffer from bad throat conditions are likely to be those who have been denied the opportunity to express themselves. I mention this example specifically because this was my own trouble when I was much younger. When once I made the space for speaking out in my life, I found I didn't get nearly as many of the dreadful cases of sore throats and strep throat. They still come back, at times, but usually when I've been in a situation where I've had to speak a lot, and to those who do not seem receptive to what I have to say. This happens a great deal at the college teaching level, I can assure you. Your ailments, also, may be a message from your body you need to receive.

When I learned to stop focusing on the "cure" for my throat ailments and stopped searching for medications that would bring relief, I was able to notice that the disease was showing me a poetry all its own, and that by understanding that message I could alter the disease. For me, the throat soreness was linked to thwarted self-expression, yes—but also to my tendency, when trying to convince others, to lean forward as I spoke, hunching my shoulders. This bodily posture actually put much more strain on my vocal chords, my lungs, and my throat. I was making myself ill. I was, physically, doing exactly the thing that would silence me—and so prevent me from having to go through the dispiriting experience of not being fully heard.

Just as soldiers in wartime developed "shell shock" (what we today would call post-traumatic stress syndrome, or PTSD), which meant that they had to be withdrawn from the front lines, so too was I, in my own way, opting to withdraw. The cure was as simple and as removed from conventional cause-and-effect thinking as one could get. Conventional wisdom said, teach less, use your voice less. What I needed, though, was self-expression. So I taught more but in a different locale, where

I knew my ideas would be fully heard. I wrote more. I stood up straighter in classes, declaring myself more fully. The throat problems evaporated.

Not all diseases are like this, obviously. Yet enough of them are similar in general outline for us to begin to see a pattern. At their most fundamental, they represent a clash between heart and head. My head tells me I have to continue in the job; my heart tells me this is destroying my soul, and I'd really rather not do it. The head over-rules the heart, at least in the short run, but eventually the body begins to show the strain, and the heart proves itself the stronger organ.

Take the time now to consider any illnesses or ailments you may have. Could you see them differently based on what we've been considering? What could your illness be trying to convey to you?

A young woman in one of my workshops who suffered from irritable bowel syndrome described how her life was spent trying to placate her parents, her much older and neglectful boyfriend, and how she was frightened of them all—and had been for years. Fear will certainly upset the stomach and bowels. It took a long time before she even admitted the possibility of a connection, and when she did her symptoms began to abate.

As she talked about her symptoms, we discovered that two other young women in the workshop were suffering in exactly the same way, although not as acutely—and fear was a large part of their lives, too. Together these three formed a support system that was nothing to do with modern medicine and everything to do with gaining a sense of personal agency. They all became better, and psychically stronger, too.

I could add examples, but they'd all point to the same thing: illness and the psyche are often linked, and the resulting disturbances will stop anyone from being able even to see flow and synchronicity, let alone access them. Instead, they'll tune into the negative flow—the place where fear creates more upset. Focusing on their negative feelings of fear, these young women had only managed to manifest more of the lack of security from which they already suffered. That's the law of attraction. When they faced their fears they no longer needed the illness to tell them what they didn't want to admit.

CHAPTER 19

The Eight Barriers
to Synchronicity

The eight barriers we've looked at so far are essential aspects of our world: the language we use, the messages we receive from the past, the way we treat our bodies, love, work, friends, family, illnesses—all are as ordinary and as vital as breath itself. They contain what makes life sweet, and also what can make it extraordinarily painful.

I'm aware that writing this critique may lead you, the reader, to feel I'm attacking all that you hold dear, or that I'm criticizing people you love, or that I'm not allowing for the fun of human differences and diversity. I'm not trying to do that. I am, however, pointing out ways that these potentially life-enhancing activities can become drains on the best part of ourselves, and you'll notice I've suggested ways we can be aware of this and also value what is good about each item.

My aim has been to point out the different ways we can be diverted from the peace and centeredness that allows us to accept the energies of the Universe, the flow that comes from the heart. It is true that what we focus on has a tendency to get bigger in our minds, but by identifying the pitfalls you can more easily avoid them. In my own life, I check in each evening with my wife, and we talk often about such potential problems—ones we see others inviting us into, and ones we've fallen into that day. We do so in the spirit that says, "Look, there's another problem area. Let's not go in that direction. Let's have compassion for those who are caught in it."

This check-in is especially useful when the people who are caught in this way are people we encounter daily. In this way, we remind ourselves of our desire to keep growing our capacity to stay at the highest emotional vibration. It also reminds us to be grateful. For we know only too well what it's like to be in that place. Perhaps it wasn't long ago that we were right there, too, and tomorrow we may be there again.

This means we accept that others may be in a different place from us, but we do not let their way of doing things upset us.

All the "faults" that I have identified and discussed in this book are real-life examples. We may see them as the actions of others to which we adapt, but let's not forget that these errors also exist in ourselves. It's just easier to see them in others. If we acknowledge that important factor, we can more easily feel compassion toward ourselves as well as others. We can let go of self-judgment as well as our judgment of others; we no longer need to blame anyone. When we do this, we free ourselves from the grip of the ego-self, which is all about judgment. The heart's way is not to judge but to forgive. First we forgive ourselves, then we forgive others—because they are just like us.

In conjunction with this wish to see the difficulties but stay in a positive space is another practice, which we need to reemphasize here. If you are to achieve your best life, it is essential to invite more of what is good into your life, and to do it daily. So create a list now of what you want more of in your life. I know—we did this earlier, but this is a very good time to revisit the exercise. Now you can try out all those ideas we've been talking about.

As you focus on what you want, you'll find it easier let go of the stuff you don't want or need. It works in exactly the same way as when you buy a new coat or some piece of clothing—it allows you to put aside the item you were wearing up to that point, which is probably looking a bit shabby. You can't wear both items at once. So you take off the old one and put on the new one.

When you make your list of what you want more of in your life, remember to be specific. Remember to apply all the insights you've gained from reading this far. You may think you want more money, when in fact what you wish for is more abundance of good things in your life. Remember the man who wished for the well-paying job? He got it, but he didn't get the peace that was the real thing he wanted. Make sure you ask for what you want.

When we ask in this way, the Universe has a tendency to supply us with what we need. This is not wishful thinking, and it's not hocus-pocus. When we know what we want, we see more clearly how much there is of what we desire right in front of our noses, and we can then strategize how to make what we need happen for us.

The man who wanted a "great wife and life partner" had to think about what that meant for him (rather than what others might tell him their version was). He decided he needed an intelligent woman who was interested in emotional and personal growth, who was also more emotionally aware than he was, who had seen the world and learned how to not take things too seriously, and who was substantially self-sufficient in emotional terms. At first he said: "I don't want a basket case," and it took some time before he could rephrase this idea in specific terms, accenting the positive. When he more precisely reformulated his wish, he began to notice that there really were women like this around; he just hadn't seen them because he'd been gazing at the leggy blondes with the great tans. The Universe had been supplying what he needed all along, but he wasn't able to see it.

It reminds me of one of my favorite lines from *My Fair Lady*, the musical version of George Bernard Shaw's play *Pygmalion*, where in one scene a garbage collector sings:

> The Lord is throwing goodness at you,
> But with a little bit of luck, a man can duck.

Perhaps we find it easier to duck, because if we catch some of that goodness then we'll have to do something with it, and often that feels like hard work. So here's what we can do to help us not to get caught up in other people's egos: We remind ourselves every day that there is another way.

Some people do this through prayer, through meditation, by doing yoga, or by practicing mind-centering exercises. These are good. The simplest, the one you can start right now, is to make a habit of daily affirmations of some sort. There are books and calendars that have a new affirmation for each day. Eileen Caddy's books work well for me. There are also plenty of organizations that offer these kinds of affirmation.

For example, Internet host Lilou Macé has created what she calls the "100-Day Challenges," in which she asks participants to commit to writing, journaling, blogging, or just checking in with their positive thoughts on a specific theme, and to do it for 100 days, every day. It's deliciously simple. And it works. If you remind yourself, every day for 100 days, that you are a worthy person who deserves respect, for example, by the end of that time you will have shifted your attitude substantially. [1]

Lilou's website is free, and there are many others like it. With a little research, anyone can find an Internet community of like-minded people, all of whom are willing to encourage each other forward, all of whom are going to do the work of writing and meditating and blogging or reading uplifting short texts, and who will be there if anyone hits a rock. You'll never have to walk alone, and by walking with others you will keep up the pace you want. Instead of asking your friends for help—those friends who may actually be part of the problem that's keeping you stuck—you can contact fellow pilgrims moving along a personal path of individual growth. It's like joining a conversation with good people whenever you need it. Every day you have a choice: go back to the same situation that kept you stuck, or find a better one.

There are plenty of easily available meditation and guided visualization tapes, many of them free. Some are to be found on the Internet through YouTube (I'm thinking of www.WellnessExperiment.com, for example), and many are excellent. For 10 minutes each day, you can listen to these meditations and emerge refreshed, and this will help to center your life and change the way you move through the world. Youtube may not be around in its present form forever, but I have no doubt that the people who supply these wonderful meditations will continue to create them. You will nurture the best parts of yourself in this way.

Some people take the next step and join an intentional community. Findhorn is just such community. Based in Scotland, it is an ecovillage, an international workshop center and a spiritual community. Others prefer to go on Pilgrim Walks through Europe, using the experience as a meditation. Still others follow a teacher or guru. Whatever feels authentic to who you are is what you should do.

These two approaches—identifying and avoiding what is bad and accepting and nurturing what is good—are essential. Often one can circumvent what is not desirable by focusing only on what is good, but not always. The Dalai Lama sent love and forgiveness to the Chinese invaders as they ravaged his land and killed his followers, but he also made sure he avoided them by fleeing to India.

The dual approach may, in fact, be an important reminder of the polarity within us. According to a verse that appears in the *Rig Veda,* two birds sit in the Tree of Life. One is tearing at the fruit, consuming it; the other sits by and observes. [2] The metaphor is deliciously simple, for both of these birds can be found within us. We are in the struggle for daily life, consuming and living, *and* we can be the detached observer. The Tree of Life requires both birds—balance. For us this means that there are times when we must flee our enemies *and* hope for their redemption. It means the rent has to be paid, *and* we need a spiritual life to make our lives worth living.

Obviously, we need to pay attention to what is inside us that is holy, and to what is outside us that is likely to hurt us. To do anything less is insufficient, and to pretend we can ignore the outside world is intellectual arrogance disguised as holiness.

If we step back from this discussion for a second, we can see that myth backs up this idea of identifying pitfalls as well as strengthening that which is holy and in the flow. The Buddha, when he was moving toward enlightenment, faced many temptations, including specifically Lust, Fear, and the customary sense of Duty. These are frequently depicted on statues of the Buddha, figures placed around him that he ignores. They are similar to what we've been considering here. We've already looked at these in terms of the problems of love and sex, self-limiting beliefs, and the demands of society and family.

Jump forward 500 years, and we see that Jesus also suffered three temptations, and they were to do with physical well-being (turning stones into bread), ambition and the political lust for power (to make all nations bow down to him), and spiritual pride (God would protect him even if he jumped from the top of the temple). The three temptations, are not the same, although we could say they're not that dissimilar. It's interesting also that when Jesus rejects the temptations he does so by quoting the words of Moses. In this way the theme of the temptation is firmly linked to the older Mosaic tradition.

This is, pretty clearly, a distinctive mythic point of change. What matters is that in all three instances, each temptation was recognized as an essential point of development, at which each person was able to identify and reject dominant cultural obsessions. In each case, these temptations threatened to keep them from being who they needed to be.

We are doing the same thing. You can slice and dice the temptations in whichever ways you need, and you can certainly have more than three categories. What's important is that the mythic structure recognizes this as a point at which we must all make decisions, so that the compassion that is in us all so abundantly can come into existence. That's what the myth can tell us, and it can guide us in our lives if we wish to use it as a point of comparison.

Obviously, we don't have to be Buddha to experience synchronicity; however, the highest forms of synchronicity are embodied in Buddha, Jesus, Moses, and others. Wonderful things happened for these figures as they went about doing important work for others. They were people with needs, of course; yet, they were serving a higher purpose. The mistake most people make when they hear about the Laws of Attraction or The Secret is that they want good things for themselves. This is very natural. It comes from the ego-space. And on the whole it doesn't work.

It's when we decide to look beyond ourselves, and become part of what the Divine needs us to do, that synchronicity can truly take an active part in our lives. When we accept our purpose as being to help the world along toward something better, then we're actually giving up our personal ambitions and handing ourselves to fate, destiny, and the Divine. "Thy will, not mine, be done" is the prayer many people offer to their specific God every day. It says all we need to know.

Before we leave this section, we need to make one more point about all these stumbling places. As we think about them, an important change can happen within us. For it is only when we step back from our experiences that we learn to see ourselves as separate from them, and even as separate from their effects. Think of it this way: try saying to yourself about your own experiences, "There is my personal history."

Then notice that you are here, commenting on it, with all the feelings you have about that history. Perhaps you can see how you are living the effects of that history into the present. Then ask yourself, who is observing these two situations?

Once you ask that question, you have acknowledged the existence of the observing part of yourself. This is the you that exists between two thoughts. This is the you that decides to step off the merry-go-round of being who you are because of the past events that shaped you. This is the you that stops buying into all the mind-traps we have spelled out so far.

This is you, getting free.

This is what it feels like to observe rather than react. It is an excellent place from which to accept synchronicity and generate more of it.

CHAPTER 20

The Necessity
of Experience

At the most basic level we need both sides of the self, the Divine and the mundane, so that we can bring our unique gifts to the world. We have a duty to our souls, but we also have a duty to contribute to the world in which we live. What does that mean, though, to contribute to the world? I think the answer is perhaps simpler than we realize.

If we are looking for meaning in the world, we may struggle. What is the meaning of a mountain? What is the meaning of a river with frogs and fish in it? We cannot ascribe words to this, or extend our minds to encompass what this might be. But we can experience these things. Even asking for "meaning" or for knowledge is a way of thinking that can only come from the ego, from the brain that wants an answer or something to carry away. Thinking that way (notice the word "thinking" immediately connects this process to the head) leaves us gazing upon the world around us as something that we can "get" something from—in this case, an answer. But if we ask the heart what these physical phenomena are worth, we're going to get a different answer, and that is that it is the experience of these things that matters.

A beautiful river or a mountain or even a mosquito that annoys you—these are all experiences that are mixed between delight and unpleasantness. The mosquito is a miracle, but it also wants to eat you and give you malaria, perhaps. We experience both aspects at the same time—the divine and the temporal, side by side. The phenomena of the outside world, so gorgeous, so mixed, so puzzling, are there to remind us of what we already know, but which we often choose to forget. We live in both worlds simultaneously. We cannot appreciate beauty without the knowledge of ugliness—and there's the mosquito reminding us. But if we spend our whole lives worrying about insects and making our homes insect-proof and taking steps to protect ourselves, we'll never move into the appreciation of the miracle of even this humblest life.

It is only by actually experiencing the world around us that we can ever come to know it. As I tell my counseling clients when they complain of having issues around trust, one learns to trust by trusting. Then trust can grow. One learns to love by loving. We may get our hearts broken a few times, but that doesn't mean the experience of heartbreak is not enrichment of the finest sort. It can be, if we wish to look at it. Which would you rather have—a heart that can be broken or the reassurance of knowing you have no heart, so it never can be broken?

I can recall only too well falling in love in my mid-twenties, and I fell very hard indeed, in the way that perhaps one can only manage at that age. The woman concerned didn't feel quite as strongly about me as I did about her, and so the affair ended. I was profoundly disappointed. I knew something had broken within me, and at the same time I was relieved because I had doubted, seriously, for some years that I could fall in love at all. I thought my heart had shriveled and died long ago. Well, there it was, hurting like hell, and it was an immense consolation to know it was still there. I knew I would recover, and go on to love again, even in the midst of my desolation.

Now, I could have chosen to withdraw from life, saying to myself that it just wasn't worth it, but instead I saw it differently. Today, I like to think of that experience as a very important one for me, yet I have nothing to "show" for it. That mysterious and beautiful dark-eyed woman did not become my life companion, but I knew I had met something within myself that to this day I find hard to articulate. The best way I can convey it is through this story. Perhaps that's the only way to communicate a flavor of it, by asking you to empathize.

The two languages of the head and the heart are so different it's astounding that we don't all suffer schizophrenic breakdowns all the time. We are asked to live in two places, and the solution is, perhaps, to live in the experience of them both.

We need to be aware of this and redress the balance. Ritual and myth used to do this for us. In my own life I realize that, quite by chance, I've been through secularized versions of some of the great rituals celebrated in other cultures. For instance, I was sent away to school in a version of the puberty rites that are part of many cultures. Like those ceremonials, I was moved from the realm of the women and mothers in my life and confined to a boarding school where we were all boys and young men together. It was a very male world, and I gained my ritual scars playing on the rugby pitch, fighting with my peers, and so on.

Through these experiences, I became independent, since there was no alternative. It was a rite of passage spread over several years, where in the case of the Masai or the

Australian aborigines it would have been a matter of days only. But in the case of these tribesmen they would know that this was a ritual—a symbolic gesturing toward something greater than themselves.

I was not quite so fortunate. I thought it was just the way things were, cruel and without redeeming value. Moreover, for the tribesmen, the ritual would be repeated every year or perhaps every several years, depending upon the population that was growing up, ready to face the ritual. And with each repetition, the depth of meaning would become more plain to those who had already passed through in previous years. They would see the new initiates and remember their own experiences, deepening their awareness, whereas the new intake would still be dazed and bewildered, until they too gained the extra insight that comes from repetition. The past, in such cases, is never over. It's always there, in the present.

It took me a long time before I could see that my experience was a ritual experience rather than just a fact. When I did, it made all the difference. For the message of the pubertal ritual is to convey basic, vital material. Young boys living in the safe world of ego with their mothers are introduced forcibly to a different world. They receive their scars, and their time of isolation as they are left to ponder who they are. In this process, their ego-selves are made subordinate to the ritual; the unconscious expressions of the dance or ceremony are experienced consciously.

After having been the little pampered princes in the women's compound, the young men now find themselves undergoing personal challenges and realize they are just the most junior members of the community of men. It reverses their previous experience. The ego, the power of thinking and living from the head, is therefore re-introduced to the heart language of the dance, the song, and what is felt in the body. The head discovers that it is useful, obviously, for certain tasks, but that the more powerful tasks can only be apprehended through the heart.

These ancient forms of ritual reestablish the primacy of the heart, which the brain and the ego are there to serve, and not the other way around. The ritual helps us to break through the daily concerns, back to the essential part of ourselves where we find we are part of the earth, not different from it. We are part of the rhythms of time and change, but we are also reconnected with the eternal as we feel this.

Now, that's all very well if you know it's a ritual and that it has a purpose. You can see the metaphor and respond to it. If you don't know, it takes longer to find any redeeming value in what's happening. In fact, the danger is that instead of the head and heart being united, the mind will put various defense mechanisms in place, which seek to deny the experience, or reduce it to an abstraction, and the vital aspect of the experience is lost. That's what happened to those boys in the boarding school. There was no mythic significance available for them. They just thought they'd been dumped in a very uncomfortable place. Instead of growing wise and compassionate, they grew resentful and brutal.

All these years later I can see the mythic aspect of the experience, but it might have been healthier for me if I could have seen them at the time, so that I could have brought the conscious world into alignment with the unconscious.

This is an extended example, but it has value. When we stop looking at our lives through the ego-lens of "this happened to me" and start seeing the patterns that link our lives to a larger context, we can let go of pain or victimhood. The ego drops away. We are all part of a pattern that is ultimately mysterious, but which human beings have acknowledged in ritual and myth for as long as anyone can compute.

This is why I have spent so much time in these pages using literature and myth. Being able to see our lives as part of this larger mythic pattern enables us to step out of the ego-space, and enter the flow, one which is as old as humanity itself.

When we respect this mythic dimension, there is far less chance that we will slip into dishonesties of thought—those occasions when we convince ourselves that "it won't matter this time." Myth shows us that there can be no such evasion, that everything has significance. The ego wants us to live in a world where all meanings are limited, where they only have relevance to us. So my lack of compassion for someone is strictly about how annoying that person is, and not about me failing to be loving. The surreptitious dumping of toxic garbage becomes just an isolated action, something that doesn't matter because no one sees it. Well, as we know, it does matter. One of the purposes of myth, as reflected in literature, is to keep the ego from taking over, and bring us back into harmony with the world we live in.

This fading of the ego into something else can be seen in a variety of places if we're prepared to look for it. I'm reminded of a young sculptor, Rebecca Warren, who was being interviewed by the *UK Guardian* newspaper. The interview was a series of questions to which brief answers were required, such as, Who is your favorite artist? What is your idea of perfect contentment? And so on. Here is how she answered some of the questions;

Do you care about fame?
A bit. Not very much.

What was the best advice anyone ever gave you?
"Stay with it, don't force it." Artist Fergal Stapleton told me this in 1992.

How would you like to be remembered?
Do I have to be remembered? [1]

That was the last response. When I read that I wanted to stand up and cheer. That's the mark of the real artist. Who cares about fame when you're doing what's vital to you? You don't care about it, no one does, because you're communicating that which feels vital for the world to know about. The doing is enough. And if you're fortunate enough to be in that space of allowing the unconscious to well up inside you, and then using your skills (which come from the head and from the body) in service of this heart work, then why worry about fame? It makes no sense. You didn't do it for the fame to begin with. At such times you are at one with yourself and at one with whatever fate has in store.

At such times one tunes in to the music of the Universe.

So go ahead and ask yourself those same questions, and see if you've got a lot of ego invested in the way you want your future to pan out. See if you can be as honest as Rebecca Warren. We all care about fame just a bit. We wouldn't be human if we didn't. It's how much space we allow it that matters.

CHAPTER 21

Channeling as a Form of Synchronicity

If we're to consider the idea of being in touch with the Universe's energy, we can't ignore the topic of channeling.

Many different types of internal voices have been identified. I've read enough, and seen enough concerning multiple personality disorders to recognize that people, especially those who have been traumatized, can sometimes split off parts of themselves that they don't even know they have. These sub-personalities can emerge in response to triggering events and take over, often without the person being fully aware that this is happening. This psychological defense to trauma certainly exists, and it is not to be confused with channeling, although I'm sure that in some cases it has been.

Many examples of channeled messages are absolutely fascinating, and full of wisdom. But I've also read extracts that have been "channeled" by people who claim to have been visited by spirits, which have caused me to wonder what is going on. A multidimensional spirit from another age would not, I sometimes feel, have such oddly contemporary grammatical infelicities. But perhaps that is just because the spirit voice has to come through a living person? A skeptic would use this as definitive proof that channeling is just a hoax; yet, I'm not so sure we can dismiss it so easily. For if our world is so convincing to us that we find it hard to embrace the transcendent, then surely it cannot be easy for the transcendent energy to communicate directly with us in words.

Countless other people have had "prophetic" dreams, in which they've seen things come true that they'd dreamed. Jung had this experience when he predicted the outbreak of the First World War, as he records in his *Red Book*. I'm sure many people saw that war coming, and yet I'm equally sure that Jung was one of the few who could see what effect it would have. Jung claims he was tuning in to the Collective Unconscious, and this seems eminently sensible. When we are connected, really connected, to the divine energies, we all become channels. [1]

I mention this because so many of the writers I've worked with over the last 20 years have said that, when they wrote, they discovered that they were wiser than they thought they were. In fact, I can think of one person who regularly rereads the book she published to remind herself of what came through those pages she wrote, and how there was more insight in them than she might otherwise have been able to access.

So what was happening here? Perhaps, when people channel a voice it may well turn out to be an aspect of their own psyche that actually is "wiser" than they themselves can manage to be. I suspect very strongly that we all have parts of ourselves that are like this. When we get out of our own way we can, very often, find the truths that would not yield themselves up to us through rational exploration. Dreams work the same way. Sometimes they are confused, and at other times they let us know the stark reality behind some event—a reality our Unconscious knows but which we can't or won't fully see in our waking consciousness. This is a type of synchronicity, too.

However we want to consider this, there is one important factor that we need to be aware of right here, and that is that when these messages arrive we are moving out of our present dimension of rational consciousness and into something else entirely. At times, there is the possibility, though not the certainty, that we contact another type of awareness. This is the Collective Unconscious, the deep wisdom of human kind that emerges into our consciousness from time to time—if we let it.

At such times we can see things clearly that others may never see. We may perceive these as visions, as voices, or as disturbing daydreams. And sometimes we see what we need to see with utter clarity. The Transcendentalist poets knew they were touching the Divine, or being touched by it, when natural beauty moved them.

For the great nineteenth century British poets William Wordsworth and Samuel Taylor Coleridge, the Divine existed in all things and was capable of breaking out in visionary moments of surprising beauty. Wordsworth called this "the still, sad music of humanity," [2] and he also referred to what he called "spots of time," [3] in which the normal rules of time and space seemed to be suspended. This was a view that was at the center of the European Romantic movement, of which the two poets were prominent exponents. They might have seen channeling as just one more example of the Divine making itself felt to those who are receptive, the god in all things making its presence known.

The popularity at that time of "automatic writing"—which was writing that was said to happen in a semi-dream state—is just another version of this. We are not watering down the idea when we see it this way; instead, we're establishing just how prevalent this has been as a human experience.

Wordsworth's sense of a permeable membrane between the ordinary world and the Divine exists in all his works. His poem "We Are Seven", published in 1798, is an encounter with a small child in a remote rural place, and the poet asks her how many brothers and sisters she has. The child insists that there are seven of them, even though several have died. The child does not differentiate between the dead and the living siblings, not because she is stupid but because the love between them has not altered. It's a startling poem in every way. [4]

Wordsworth was not the first poet to feel this way, of course, but he was one of the first in modern times to go out on a limb and say what he perceived. Before him the great poet and political activist John Milton was in the habit of going on lengthy fasts in order to induce visions and otherworldly experiences, which he felt were close to flying. And his contemporary, Andrew Marvell, refers in one of his greatest poems, "The Garden," to an out-of-body experience of great peace and beauty.

> Here at the fountain's sliding foot,
> Or at some fruit-tree's mossy root,
> Casting the body's vest aside,
> My soul into the boughs does glide:
> There like a bird it sits and sings,
> Then whets and combs its silver wings,
> And, till prepared for longer flight,
> Waves in its plumes the various light. [5]

As his soul separates from his body, temporarily, it sits in the tree like a bird getting ready for a longer flight—which would presumably be when the poet dies—and he feels no fear or trepidation.

Marvell was alive and writing in a world of seventeenth-century Christian orthodoxy, which meant the possibility of being judged and sent to Hell for blasphemy would have been very real to him. Yet Marvell wrote what he felt. Remember, this was a poet who had already spent considerable amounts of time writing poems about the inner dialogue each person has within him or herself—dialogues we could easily sum up as the struggle of the ego with the heart. Marvell was a practical politician, though, and so his poems always end in a hung jury—the beauty of the eternal is yearned for, but the purely factual needs of the day seem to demand that we give into them.

It would be possible to add many poets and writers to this discussion, but that would be less important than to acknowledge that poets are not quite like other people in this respect. Deepak Chopra has stated on several occasions that he and Wayne Dyer agreed on many things, including that poets "go to the heart of creation".[6] It's a sentiment that Joseph Campbell also shared and repeated on many occasions. Poets are the ones who are able to articulate the experiences that exist beyond the normal scope of words. This connection with the Divine is at the center of synchronicity.

What we can take from this is that visionary experience is far more commonly recorded than we think. It's just that for the past 200 years, the "rational" ego experience has been held up as being more valuable, more important. And so the great writers have been silenced, often by those who have simply ignored their messages or tried to explain them away. That era is now ending.

I'd like to go one step farther and say that most human beings yearn for this type of connection, for something larger; we long to touch the Divine. We find it regularly in public performances of music, plays, and so on. Drama is precious to us because in it we see actors, perhaps playing people who look like everyday individuals, moving through a pattern that can show us something we hadn't seen or known about before. As they do so, if the performance and the play is any good, we feel emotions that are like our own and simultaneously larger than we are, connecting us to something transpersonal. The divine breaks through, and we are moved, we feel more alive, and we are reminded that living is a richer experience than we routinely acknowledge in our busy lives.

Why is it, then, that we confine this experience to only "acceptable" places like theaters? I think it's because the rational world of our day job that pays the rent has got the upper hand over our internal visionary world that has a hard time making any payment at all. It is this imbalance that has to change if the world is to change. It is worthwhile, as visionary poet William Blake said in *Auguries of Innocence*:

> To see a world in a grain of sand,
> And a heaven in a wild flower,
> Hold infinity in the palm of your hand,
> And eternity in an hour.[7]

We can do this any time we like, if we wish. We can look at that grain of sand and move away from the diurnal rut of grinding facts. We can be aware of the unpleasant things on the earth and yet see the magnificent things—things that touch our hearts and put us in contact with eternity. But we can't put them on our resume and expect to get a job. At least not yet.

When we exist in harmonious acceptance of Nature and the seasons—which after all is what myths are supposed to help us do, to let us feel there is a shape to our lives—when we do that, we can see through the activities of everyday and find the eternal in them. At that point everything is capable of becoming holy, and everything can be a prayer. Doing the dishes can be a meditative act. Surely, harsh things happen. Creatures kill and devour each other, sickness arrives and so does suffering, but if we see these events as inevitable consequences of being alive they don't have the same power to unnerve us. Decay, disease, and death are what happen to every human being—but we aren't about to give up being alive just because of that. Otherwise, we'd all give up when we suffer our first bout of flu.

Our fate is to die. Our destiny is not to know with any certainty what our actions may create later in the course of things, when we are dead. The demand upon us, therefore, is to be in this world with all its imperfections, all its temptations, and still behave the best we can possibly manage.

This brings us back to the question, where does this channeled wisdom come from, and why is it so perplexing, sometimes? There may be an answer. The wisdom we receive, the voices some of us hear, may come from the cosmos or from God, who is to say? But one thing we can say, and that is that when we are attuned to the cosmos, when the ego-state is diminished, then what we can attain is what Eileen Caddy called "the God within you," and which Buddhists call "the Divine within you." When operating out of that place of centeredness, what matters is that we listen to what is said.

Eileen Caddy is very specific when she explains channeling. She asked fellow channel David Spangler to ask his higher sensitivity, "John," for an explanation about the voice she was hearing. This is what emerged:

> The voice you hear is an amalgam of your own consciousness and
> the source. What you hear is not the source but its servant. Now
> you yourself must expand and grow so that your relationship
> with your source, a life energy inexpressible in words, can grow.
> Out of that relationship shall come a new voice, or perhaps a
> fuller communication.
>
> God is not an abstract but a relationship. [...] Behind the
> voice, then, is a source which is your true nature, which you are
> seeking to grow into ever more fully. [8]

What this tells us is that the voice of the Source, the primal energy of the Universe, can only reach us in forms we are able to hear at the level of awareness we are living in. This means that to some extent we, all of us, have the experience of God that we are capable of imagining. The difficulty for us, as humans, is that the God we have in our imaginations may be the very thing that actually stops us from seeing and hearing the Divine. We like the things we like about the version of God we have now, and we want to hold on to them.

As our awareness expands, we may find that our version of God is no longer large enough to comprehend what the Divine might be. In this, we have to remind ourselves of the saying "When I was a child... I thought as a child; but when I became a man I put away childish things."[9] We have to put away these habits and the things that we have outgrown, and we may have to do that over and over, just as we have to put aside our version of God or the Divine energy that we have outgrown so we can let the higher version into our lives.

Some channeling experiences may well be hard to comprehend, if we are simply observers, because in essence they are private communications between the particular version of God within and the person concerned. We can learn from them, but ultimately they are often individual lessons, spiritual teachings aimed at one person and tailored to bring that person forward one step at a time. They exist as one person's heart tuning in to the Divine, and that wisdom talking to that specific person; and as we have seen, the heart wisdom is activated fully only when it is in tune with the energy of the Universe. It is a version of synchronicity.

CHAPTER 22

The Nature of the Journey Ahead

Perhaps the only conclusion to a book like this is to consider that the way forward, for all of us, can have no specific destination. There is no endpoint that we will be able to identify. So the nature of what we do with our lives must, therefore, have to do with who we are now—and that means we must be constantly in a state of becoming. When seen this way the journey through our lives becomes even more interesting, because we know there will always be more doorways to open and more profound things to explore. The real end is the journey itself, and we can't lose our way as long as we follow our authentic bliss, our inner prompting.

We know what this feels like, and we know we cannot be diverted from it for very long. We yearn to get back to it. For in that space, we are who we are supposed to be. Synchronicity and the "coincidences" provided by the guiding hand let us know that we are on the right path, as they guide us on toward the next step we need to take. They reassure us as well as help us. But when we stray from the path where the energy of another dimension can reach us, we stop receiving synchronous events, we stop feeling the freedom that comes from truly being in the flow, and we know we've drifted from where we need to be.

If we're alert to this, the answer is fairly simple: We have to ask ourselves what caused us to get off course and try to remove that interference. We are like radio sets or old-fashioned television sets with antennae, you might say. We receive these messages from elsewhere, messages we can't see, but we then can make them perceivable through our consciousness. And when the transmission is upset because we've tuned our internal receivers to the wrong frequency, then the picture goes, the music stops, and all we get are interference lines and a loud hiss of static. If we are sensitive to this we can't go far wrong. The energy will guide us. It always has.

Now, a little over a hundred years ago, if I'd used that comparison to radio and television waves people would have thought I was crazy. Such things could not be! Voices coming through the air without wires! Pictures broadcast over the ether? What nonsense! Today, we know it can and does happen. Perhaps in a hundred years, we'll have another language that explains how the Guiding Hand works, and it will be seen as every bit as ordinary. Who knows? And it doesn't actually matter. We need to use what comes to us, not argue about the mechanism by which it arrives. We use gravity everyday and yet no one fully understands that. Eckhart Tolle is delightfully eloquent about this:

> You are not just a meaningless fragment in an alien universe,
> briefly suspended between life and death, allowed a few short-
> lived pleasures followed by pain and ultimate annihilation.
> Underneath your outer form, you are connected with something
> so vast, so immeasurable and sacred, that it cannot be spoken
> of—yet I am speaking of it now. I am speaking of it now not to
> give you something to believe in but to show you how you can
> know it for yourself. [1]

Here's Rumi, with advice that will help us all.

> Keep walking, though there's no place to get to.
> Don't try to see through the distances.
> That's not for human beings. Move within,
> But don't move the way fear makes you move. [2]

In the end, synchronicity is a way, a series of prompts, along the path to what we may never achieve, but which is still a worthy goal. When we've purged ourselves of the errors we've examined in these pages, (and perhaps a few more, as well, specific to each of us), when we've let go of ego and replaced that swirling aspect of our desires with compassion, understanding, and deep acceptance, then we will know what our immortal nature is. At that point, we can realize our union with the Eternal Being. Synchronicity, at that moment, is complete.

Afterword

While writing this book, I was aware of the many synchronicities and inspirations that came to guide me along the way. Material seemed to pop up wherever I went—if I was prepared to listen for it and welcome it into my life. This was reassuring, since to write a book about synchronicity, and not to feel its presence in my life everyday, would have seemed like pushing a truckload of rocks up a steep sandy hill—that would have felt like force rather than flow. I had no intention of working against my own observations and principles.

Since so much of what appears here is backed up by what others have said and thought, at times, I found myself wondering if I was simply repeating large segments of what, in different ways, had been said before by others and which I had absorbed over a lifetime. This may be true. All I can say is that this is not new knowledge. This idea of the interweaving of fate, the Guiding Hand of the Universe, synchronicity, luck, and our personal role in adding to our own luck—these are not new concepts; they are as old as humanity. It also is painfully apparent that we've forgotten much of what was once hard-won knowledge about such things and need to be reminded, so that we do not fall into the ego traps that are so plentifully present for all of us.

When viewed from the outside, those who are in the flow of synchronicity may look as if they are the chosen ones of God, or Fate, the blessed ones of our world. From the inside, though, those who have experienced synchronicity will tell you it takes work, devotion, and alertness. It requires us to listen and remain calm in the face of uncertainty. It requires sacrifice—if giving up the rewards of the ego world can be seen as sacrifice. It will provide a deep sense of joy, though, that is superior by far to any physical item we can own, lust after, or want in our own possession. Being there is the reward.

Introduction

1. "The dark night of the soul" is a phrase attributed to the 16th-century Spanish poet and Roman Catholic mystic St. John of the Cross.

Chapter 1

1. Vonnegut's quotation is from *Bluebeard* (New York: Delacorte, 1987), p. 216, and the character is Rabo Karabekian.
2. The Deepak Chopra interview with Jean Huston was recorded at La Costa, California. 3/1/10. See: www.Youtube.com/watch?v=3pfO2X5An4s

Chapter 2

1. Arthur Schopenhauer. "Transcendent Speculation on the Apparent Deliberateness in the Fate of the Individual" (1851). Reprinted in *Parerga and Paralipomena: Short Philosophical Essays*. Volume 1 (Cary, NC: Oxford University Press USA, 2001).
2. The story of Robert the Bruce is widely recounted.
3. For the story of Tamerlane, please see: *http://www.silkroaddestinations.com/uzbekistan.html#shz*.
4. The tale of Alfred and the burned cakes was first recorded in the 12th century and is so popular it even appears on the British Royal Family's official website: *http://www.royal.gov.uk/HistoryoftheMonarchy/KingsandQueensofEngland/TheAnglo-Saxonkings/AlfredtheGreat.aspx*

Chapter 3

1. For further information, please see the article by John Chitty, RPP, RCST, *The Heart Is Not (Just) a Pump, www.energyschoolcom/CSES_Home/Resources_files/heartpump.pdf*

2. *The Bhagavad Gita*. Translated by Eknath Easwaran. (Tomales, CA: Nilgiri Press, 1985), section 3:9, p.105.

3. Joseph Campbell, *The Wisdom of Joseph Campbell*, New Dimensions audio CD set (California: Hay House, 1997).

4. Baptist de Pape interview; reported conversation by Baptist, 2009.

5. Eric Maisel. *Fearless Creating: A Step By Step Guide to Creating and Completing Your Work of Art* (Los Angeles: Tarcher, 1995).

6. Andrew Cohen, quoted by Michael Wombacher. *11 Days at the Edge* (Scotland: Findhorn Press, 2008).

Chapter 4

1. Patti Smith, *Just Kids* (New York: HarperCollins, 2010), p.240.

Chapter 5

1. Alan Cohen, widely reprinted quotation.

2. Ibid. See also: *http://weboflife.org.uk/wiki/Quotes/WordsToLightYourWay*.

3. A short and clear exposition of karma and dharma is to be found in an article by Einar Adalsteinsson, Theosophical Society in Iceland, June 1996, *www.gudspekifelagid.is*. I am indebted to Thierry Bogliolo for bringing this to my attention. A fuller exposition is to be found in *The Dhammapada*, translated by Eknath Easwaran (Tomales, CA: Nilgiri Press, 1985). The introduction is excellent.

Chapter 7

1. Sticky Hair. For a fuller version of this tale see: Joseph Campbell, *The Hero with a Thousand Faces* (Princeton, NJ: University Press, 1973), p. 85-89. In this version, Prince Five Weapons calls the power within him "a thunderbolt," which is to be understood as the power of knowledge that all things are not merely physical.

2. The quotation is from the Warner Brothers' trailer for *Harry Potter and the Deathly Hallows*, 2010.

3. Joe Simpson. *Touching the Void: The True Story of One Man's Miraculous Survival* (New York: Perennial, 2004).

Chapter 8

1. Inanna and Ereshkigal. The myth appears in S. N. Kramer, *Sumerian Mythology*, American Philosophical Society Memoirs, Vol. XXI; Philadelphia, 1944. p. 86-93. Sumerian mythology is important in this discussion since it is the source of Babylonian, Assyrian, Phoenician, and Biblical traditions. See also: Joseph Campbell, *The Hero with a Thousand Faces*, p.108. Campbell argues that Inanna is the model for a string of later goddesses—Ishtar, Astarte, Aphrodite, and Venus, op. cit., p.213–214.
2. See: Joseph Campbell, The New Dimensions Media CD set, op. cit.
3. Rumi. *The Book of Love*. Translated by Coleman Barks (HarperSanFrancisco, 2003), p.123. All Rumi references are from this excellent edition.

Chapter 9

1. The Eleusinian Mysteries are described here as depicted on the Pietro Asa Bowl, interpreted by Joseph Campbell, in his masterful exposition in *Mythos I*, disk 2, PBS series, 1996 and 2007.
2. Recently, I watched a rerun of the Sandra Bullock movie *Speed*, first produced by Twentieth Century Fox in 1994. In it, the villain is a good-cop-gone-bad (the Shadow is a reflection of our negative impulses) who takes the hero and heroine on a wild chase that ends with a descent into the subway system (i.e. the Underworld). There the bad cop is killed, and the unflappable good cop (Keanu Reeves) manages to save himself and Sandra Bullock and is romantically united with her in an animus-finds-anima echo. It's a familiar mythic pattern, reworked.

Chapter 10

1. Eileen Caddy. *God Spoke To Me* (Scotland: Findhorn Press, 1992). p.31.
2. Virgil. *Aeneid*, VI, 892. There are many excellent translations. This one is from: http://www.poetryintranslation.com/PITBR/Latin/VirgilAeneidVI.htm#_Toc2242944
3. Deepak Chopra, in conversation, reported by Baptist de Pape.
4. Wayne Dyer; the quotation is from his website *http://www.drwaynedyer.com/articles/you-are-god-an-in-depth-conversation-with-dr-wayne-dyer*
5. "Born Under a Bad Sign" lyrics by William Bell and Booker T. Jones, originally recorded by Albert King. Cream recorded their version in 1968.

Chapter 11

1. Cat Bennett. *The Confident Creative: Drawing to Free the Hand and Mind* (Scotland: Findhorn Press, 2010).
2. Anne Lamott. *Bird By Bird: Some Instructions on Writing and Life* (New York: Anchor Press, 1995). Lamott's phrase "really shitty first drafts" also appears in Lisa Garrigues, *Writing Motherhood* (New York: Scribner, 2008), p.168.
3. *The World's Fastest Indian*, directed by Roger Donaldson, starring Anthony Hopkins (Magnolia Pictures, 2005).
4. Joseph Campbell referred frequently to "the call" in his many lectures and books. Once again, I can do no better than to refer the interested reader to his four-CD set *The Wisdom of Joseph Campbell* (New Dimensions Media, 1997), which contains the highlights of over a dozen years of interviews with Campbell.
5. Carlos Ruiz Zafor. *The Shadow of the Wind* (New York: Penguin, 2005), p.444.
6. The Ursula Le Guin quote has been widely recorded; see: *http://www.goodreads.com/author/quotes/874602.Ursula_K_Le_Guin*.
7. The story of Jonah and the whale and his time in Nineveh is in *The Book of Jonah*, chapters 1–3.
8. "The Holy Land Experience" is meticulously documented in Wikipedia. I am grateful to Nicky Leach, who wrote a travel piece on it, for drawing it to my attention. The Creation Museum, Ky., is documented in many online websites and reviews. It all makes for fascinating reading.
9. William Shakespeare. *Hamlet*, Act V, Scene 2, lines 10–11.

Chapter 12

1. Rumi. *The Book Of Love*, op. cit., p.146.

Chapter 13

1. William Shakespeare. *Hamlet*, Act 2, Scene 2, line 246.
2. John Lennon's words are from his single, "Watching the Wheels," released posthumously in 1981.

Chapter 14

1. "Little Red-Cap," as discussed here, is the version that appears in *The Complete Grimm's Fairy Tales* (New York: Pantheon, 1972). This is the finest edition of the tales available.
2. Howard Thurman. This quotation is widely reproduced, including in Wikipedia. The exact page reference in Thurman's works is not known.
3. Oprah Winfrey. *O, The Oprah Magazine*, 13 October 2009, "What I Know for Sure." The quotation also appears on her website: *http://www.oprah.com/omagazine/What-Oprah-Knows-for-Sure-About-Destiny*.

Chapter 15

1. Here is what Nicky Leach, a highly skilled craniosacral therapist, has to say about this process of shaking off negative energy: "Animals deactivate the sympathetic nervous system by physically shaking off the adrenaline and returning to the parasympathetic state; humans, with their higher brain overriding natural responses, stay in an activated sympathetic state unless they do something tangible and physical like an animal to get rid of it." This idea is explored in detail by Peter Levine in *Waking the Tiger: Healing Trauma*, (North Atlantic Books, 1997), which is about post-traumatic stress disorder and stress.
2. Charles Swindoll quotation is from *Attitudes* (Grand Rapids: Zondervan, 1995) and has been widely repeated elsewhere.
3. W.H. Murray. *The Scottish Himalayan Expedition* (1951), unknown publisher. This quotation has been widely circulated and is also cited by Julia Cameron in *The Artist's Way*, (Los Angeles: Tarcher, 1992). See also: *http://www.goethesociety.org/pages/quotescom.html*

Chapter 16

1. Thich Nhat Hanh. *Peace Is Every Step: The Path of Mindfulness in Everyday Life* (New York: Bantam, 1992).

Chapter 17

1. Christian D. Larson. *Your Forces and How to Use Them.* (Nabu Press, 1912, reprinted 2010), p. 21.
2. Eileen Caddy. *God Spoke To Me*, op. cit., p.83.

Chapter 18

1. Dr. Christiane Northrup. *Women's Bodies, Women's Wisdom: Creating Physical and Emotional Health and Healing.* Third Edition. (New York: Bantam, 2006).
2. Louise Hay. *You Can Heal Your Life.* (Carlsbad: Hay House, 2005).

Chapter 19

1. Lilou Macé, *http://www.cocreatingourreality.com*
2. *The Rig Veda.* Translated by Ralph T. H. Griffith, 1896. Reprint (Forgotten Books, 2008), Book 1, Hymn 164, verses 20-22.
3. The words of Moses are quoted from *Deuteronomy* 6:16, where he refers to the Jews at Massah, which is an episode described in *Exodus* 17:5.

Chapter 20

1. Rebecca Warren Interview, *The Guardian*, by Laura Barnett, 7 April 2009. *www.guardian.co.uk/artanddesign/2009/apr/07/sculptor-rebecca-warren*

Chapter 21

1. The interested reader would do well to look at the writing of biologist Rupert Sheldrake, who gives the name "morphic resonance" to this phenomenon.
2. "The still sad music of humanity" is from William Wordsworth, "Tintern Abbey," line 91, composed 13 July 1798.
3. "Spots of time" is from William Wordsworth, "The Prelude," book 12, line 208, 1805 edition.
4. "We are Seven" appeared in *Lyrical Ballads* (1798).
5. Andrew Marvell. "The Garden," stanzas six and seven.
6. Deepak Chopra. "'How to Get what You Really Want" Part 7. See: *Youtube. com/watch?v=o79gCTCjdu.* Recorded December 2008.
7. William Blake. "Auguries of Innocence," widely reprinted. The poem was composed in 1803.
8. Eileen Caddy. *Flight into Freedom,* (Scotland: Findhorn Press, 2002), p.196
9. The Bible. *1 Corinthians, 13:11.*

Chapter 22

1. Eckhart Tolle. *The Power of Now: A Guide to Spiritual Enlightenment* (Novato: New World Library, 2004). The quotation also appears on various websites including: *http://peacefulrivers.homestead.com/EckhartTolle.html*
2. Rumi, op. cit., p.149.

Adalsteinsson, Einar. "Dharma and Kharma." Theosophical Society in Iceland, June 1996. www.gudspekifelagid.is.

Bhagavad Gita, The. Translated by Eknath Easwaran. Tomales, CA: Nilgiri Press, 1985.

Caddy, Eileen. *God Spoke To Me.* Scotland: Findhorn Press, 1992.
    Flight into Freedom. Scotland: Findhorn Press, 2002.
Campbell, Joseph. *The Wisdom of Joseph Campbell.* New Dimensions CD set. Carlsbad, CA: Hay House, 1997.
    The Hero with a Thousand Faces. New Jersey: Princeton University Press, reprint,1968.
Csikszentmihalyi, Mihaly, *Creativity: Flow and the Psychology of Discovery and Invention.* New York: Harper Perennial, 1997.
    Finding Flow: The Psychology of Engagement with Daily Life. New York: Basic Books, 1998.
The Complete Grimm's Fairy Tales. New York: Pantheon, 1944 and 1972.

Dhammapada, The. Translated by Eknath Easwaran. Tomales, CA: Nilgiri Press, 1985.

Hay, Louise. *You Can Heal Your Life,* Carlsbad, CA: Hay House, 1984.
Hunter, Allan G. *Princes, Frogs and Ugly Sisters: The Healing Power of the Grimm Brothers' Tales.* Scotland: Findhorn Press, 2010.

Maisel, Eric. *Fearless Creating: A Step By Step Guide to Creating and Completing Your Work of Art.* Los Angeles, CA: J. P. Tarcher, 1995.
Myss, Caroline. *Anatomy of the Spirit: The Seven Stages of Power and Healing.* New York: Three Rivers Press, 1997.

Northrup, Christiane. *Women's Bodies, Women's Wisdom.* New York: Bantam (new edition) 2010.

Rumi. *The Book of Love.* Translated by Coleman Barks. San Francisco, CA: HarperSanFrancisco, 2003.

Schopenhauer, Arthur. "Transcendent Speculation on the Apparent Deliberateness in the Fate of the Individual" (1851). Reprinted in *Parerga and Paralipomena: Short Philosophical Essays.* Volume 1. Cary, NC: Oxford University Press USA, 2001.
Simpson, Joe. *Touching the Void: The True Story of One Man's Miraculous Survival.* New York: Perennial, 2004 (revised edition).

Smith, Patti. *Just Kids*. New York: HarperCollins, 2010.

Thich Nhat Hanh. *Peace Is Every Step*: *The Path of Mindfulness in Everyday Life*. New York: Bantam, 1992.

Tolle, Eckhart. *The Power of Now*: *A Guide to Spiritual Enlightenment*. New York: New World Library, 2004.

About the Author

Allan G. Hunter was born in England in 1955 and completed all his degrees at Oxford University, emerging with a doctorate in English Literature in 1983. His first book was *Joseph Conrad and the Ethics of Darwinism*. In 1986, after working at Fairleigh Dickinson University's British campus and at Peper Harow Therapeutic Community for disturbed adolescents, he moved to the US. For the past twenty years, he has been a professor of literature at Curry College in Massachusetts, and a therapist. He has produced two books specifically aimed at using writing and drawing exercises therapeutically - *The Sanity Manual* and *Life Passages*. Both books are based on his revolutionary interactive writing exercises, tried and proven in counselling sessions and classes. While working with clients in this way, he began to uncover the presence of a series of archetypes within their writings. This led to his present work with the formulation of the six archetypal stages of spiritual development.

Four years ago, he began teaching with the Blue Hills Writing Institute and he has remained with it ever since, working with students to explore the memoir and life-writing. His own experience of this medium is reflected in *From Coastal Command to Captivity; The Memoir of a Second World War Airman*, a project on which he worked with his father up to the time of his death. It required extensive reworking to bring this memoir to completion. As in all his books, the emphasis is on the healing nature of the stories we weave for ourselves if we choose to connect to the archetypal tales of our culture.

For further information, see *http://allanhunter.net/*

Further Allan G. Hunter titles

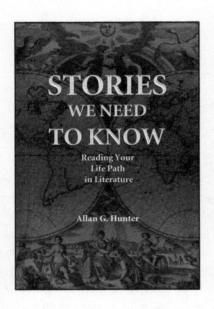
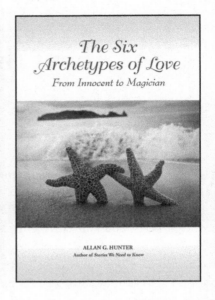

STORIES WE NEED TO KNOW

If you're looking for reliable, time-tested guidance on your journey through life then this is the book for you. Using the wisdom of over three thousand years of literature and myth, Dr. Allan Hunter explores the stories we need to know and understand, and shows how they have offered us real advice and guidance for generations.

978-1-84409-123-2

THE SIX ARCHETYPES OF LOVE

Dr. Allan G. Hunter identifies six classic profiles of individuals in love; the Innocent, the Orphan, the Pilgrim, the Warrior-Lover, the Monarch and the Magician. He shows how we can move through and become any one of these archetypes at different stages in our lives and our spiritual development.

978-1-84409-142-3

Further Allan G. Hunter titles

WRITE YOUR MEMOIR

Extending beyond the idea that memoir writing is intended to put past events into a more understandable current perspective, this guide maintains that keeping a document of one's life is actually the basis of a psychic process called "soul work," which manifests as a desire to experience the state of being alive to the fullest.

978-1-84409-177-5

PRINCES, FROGS & UGLY SISTERS

Discover the difference between what the Grimm brothers' tales actually say and what we think they ought to have said, and in the process find real, vital insights into how we could live more happily, understand our need for personal growth, and find our significant other.

978-1-84409-184-3

FINDHORN PRESS

Life-Changing Books

Consult our catalogue online
(with secure order facility) on
www.findhornpress.com

For information on the Findhorn Foundation:
www.findhorn.org